PRAISE FOR HEALTHY HUSTLE

'*Healthy Hustle* is a game-changer for business owners and leaders. Nicky and Vanessa have masterfully combined practical strategies with insightful stories to guide you from chaos to clarity. Their approach to smart growth and peak performance is both refreshing and actionable. This book will help you lead your business to new heights while reclaiming your time and energy.'

– Donna McGeorge, Best-selling author and global authority on productivity

'*Healthy Hustle* is groundbreaking for business leaders and entrepreneurs alike. It provides practical, actionable steps to achieve peak performance in business while maintaining balance and wellbeing. The book is packed with insights on leadership, team dynamics, and productivity that are both inspiring and easy to implement. Whether you're looking to transform your business, optimise your team's performance, or simply find a better work-life balance, this book is an invaluable resource.

This dynamic duo have distilled years of experience and wisdom into a comprehensive guide that teaches how to shift from the traditional, exhausting hustle to a more sustainable, healthy approach to business growth.'

– James Bartrop, Founder and Managing Director ShadowSafe

'Over the past decade, I've seen Nicky and Ness's strategies develop into a powerful toolkit yielding exceptional results. *Healthy Hustle* offers a clear, prioritised roadmap to guide leaders from chaos to clarity. Their innovative, actionable methods for smart growth and peak performance are transformative. I've applied these strategies, including in digital transformation, with great success. This book is essential for business owners and senior leaders seeking to optimise time and preserve energy for ALL the moments that matter.'

– Gemma Visentin, Cross Functional Corporate Expert & Leader

'*Healthy Hustle* by Nicky and Ness is a game-changer for business leaders who have flirted with burnout while chasing success. As someone who has nearly hit the wall multiple times, this book is a revelation. It debunks the myth that long hours are the key to achievement and instead offers a practical blueprint for working smarter, not harder. If you're a business leader who wants to build a thriving team without sacrificing your wellbeing, this is a must-read guide.'

– **Leah Mether**, Communication speaker and trainer. Global authority and author of the acclaimed books Steer Through the Storm and Soft is the New Hard

'Nicky and Ness have the antidote to grind culture that'll shake you out of the hustle into a truly sustainable way of working. This book blends humour and wisdom with a spot of cheekiness that's just so them. You'll laugh, you'll think, and—most importantly—you'll be inspired to act. Backed by evidence that'll convince even the most resistant among us, this page-turner leaves you no place to hide. Prepare to unlearn old habits, relearn new ones, and develop a healthier approach to business and life.'

– **Karen Tisdell**, LinkedIn Profile Writer, Trainer and Speaker

'*Healthy Hustle* is a refreshing and insightful guide for business owners and corporate leaders who have already achieved a level of success or for those starting out and looking for tools to guide them on their journey.

One of the standout features of *Healthy Hustle* is its focus on working smarter rather than harder. This is a book that recognises the pitfalls of the relentless hustle culture, offering instead a balanced approach that prioritises efficiency and effectiveness.

Its practical tools and strategies are grounded in real-world application, making it a valuable resource for anyone looking to sustain long-term success without sacrificing their quality of life.'

– **Joe Visentin**, National Sales Manager at Canon Australia

Healthy
HUSTLE

Healthy HUSTLE

The New Blueprint to Thrive in Business and Life

BY NICKY MIKLÓS
WITH VANESSA MEDLING

NICKY *Miklós*

Production Credits:

Edited by Stephanie Preston

Proofread by Tania Favazza

Book coach: Kelly Irving

Typeset by Zoë deBlank

Cover design by Ellie Schroeder

Interior layout design by Ellie Schroeder

Printed and bound by Ingram Sparks and Lulu.

Disclaimer:

The material in this publication is of the nature of general comment only and does not represent professional advice. It is not intended to provide specific guidance for particular circumstances, and it should not be relied on as the basis for any decision to take action or not take action on any matter which it covers. Readers should obtain professional advice where appropriate, before making any such decision. To the maximum extent permitted by law, the author and publisher disclaim all responsibility and liability to any person, arising directly or indirectly from any person taking or not taking action based on the information in this publication.

National Library of Australia Cataloguing-in-Publication entry

Title: Healthy Hustle

Subtitle: The New Blueprint to Thrive in Business and Life

ISBN: 978-0-646-70075-5 (paperback)
ISBN: 978-1-7636847-1-3 (audiobook)
ISBN: 978-1-7636847-0-6 (e-book)

Subjects: Business, leadership, self-care.

To the bold business owners and visionary leaders who are the true change agents.

This book is for those who are driven by passion, committed to success, and determined to achieve it without sacrificing their wellbeing.

You are the pioneers who are not only building impactful businesses but are also redefining what it means to lead with purpose, balance, and heart.

Our hope is that this book will play a small part in changing the business landscape for a better, more sustainable way of thriving in both business and life.

CONTENTS

ABOUT
The Authors

Nicky and Ness are seasoned business leaders and coaches, dedicated to transforming the way business owners approach growth and success. With over fifty years of combined experience in leadership, sales, and coaching, they bring a wealth of knowledge and a unique perspective to the table. Both have successfully run coaching businesses since 2015, and together they co-founded Business Together, a venture that helped business owners break free from the relentless cycle of busyness and build businesses by design.

Nicky is a TEDx speaker whose journey is one of resilience and reinvention. After experiencing burnout in 2012, she redefined her approach to success, shifting from relentless hustle to sustainable growth. This pivotal moment fuelled her passion for helping others achieve balance and fulfilment in both business and life. Her mission is to empower business owners to step back from chaos, unlock their potential, and create thriving businesses that can stand strong, even in their absence. Today, Nicky continues this work by partnering with businesses to activate sustainable sales growth, build strong leadership capability, and help high performers find their own sweet spot of healthy hustle through speaking engagements, facilitating training programs, and coaching.

Ness brings a deep understanding of human behaviour and a genuine care for helping others reach their full potential. After a successful career in executive leadership, she transitioned into coaching, driven by a passion for helping others create success on their own terms. She is particularly passionate about financial self-reliance, especially for women. She is an experienced coach, mentor, and facilitator, known for her engaging and inspirational style that leaves a lasting impact.

If you're into the formal stuff, you might like to know that both Nicky and Ness are accredited in eDISC Behavioral Profiling, are Meta Dynamics Level 3 Practitioners of Neuro-Linguistic Programming (NLP) and are qualified Professional Coaches and Facilitators.

When they're not busy transforming businesses, you'll find Nicky enjoying walks with her wife, Jules, and their three dogs, or getting lost in a DanceFiit class. Ness loves spending quality time with her grown-up kids, Cam and Bec, her partner Wayne, and spoiling her Spoodle, Charlie.

A Note from the Authors

While much of the writing and personal stories in *Healthy Hustle* come from Nicky's pen, the wisdom, insights, and practical tools shared throughout these pages are a true collaboration.

This book is born from the combined experience, intellectual property, and client work that both Nicky and Ness have passionately cultivated over the years.

Every strategy and piece of advice you'll find here is a reflection of their shared journey in transforming businesses and lives. Together, they've distilled decades of knowledge into a blueprint for success that blends the best of their individual and collective expertise.

FOREWORD

By Janine Garner

You've heard the drill a thousand times: "In the event of an emergency, an oxygen mask will drop from the compartment above. Fit your mask on first before assisting others." It's an instruction we all know by heart, but how many of us actually heed that advice in the chaos of our daily lives? I'm willing to bet that most of us, when faced with real-life emergencies – or even just the relentless demands of our daily grind – would instinctively reach to help someone else first.

This instinct to prioritise others over ourselves isn't just ingrained in our biology – it's been reinforced by society, culture, and even the endless stream of advertising we're bombarded with. We're taught that self-care is selfish, that the only way to reach the top is to keep pushing, keep going, keep sacrificing. But here's the truth: Busy isn't leadership. Burnout isn't success.

That's why *Healthy Hustle* is such a crucial read for anyone who's ever felt the weight of the world on their shoulders. This book is not just a collection of strategies for growing your business; it's a blueprint for thriving in every aspect of your life. It challenges the outdated notion that success requires relentless sacrifice and introduces a new paradigm where smart growth, peak performance, and time freedom coexist in harmony. This is not just theory – it's a proven approach, backed by real-life examples of individuals who have not only grown their businesses but have also reclaimed their lives in the process.

Take the story of Michelle and Douglas, who dared to ask themselves a question most business owners wouldn't even entertain: What if we stepped away from our business for a year? Could it survive without us? Their journey, from doubting the possibility to empowering their team and ultimately thriving during their time abroad, is a powerful testament to the ideas laid out in this book. They didn't just grow their business; they grew as individuals and as a family, discovering that true success isn't about how much you do, but about how well you align your business with your life.

Healthy Hustle is packed with practical tools, actionable strategies, and real-world stories like Michelle and Douglas's. It's about understanding the difference between chaos that drives innovation and growth, and chaos that leads to burnout and decline. With the insights in this book, you'll learn how to create an environment where you and your team can thrive without being tethered to the daily grind.

The old-school hustle – where we push ourselves to the brink – doesn't have to be the only path to success. In fact, it's often the most dangerous one. I used to believe the same stories you might be telling yourself now – stories that justified the constant doing, the never-ending to-do lists, and the relentless pursuit of more. But those stories were just excuses, masking the real problem: I wasn't prioritising my own well-being.

Putting your own needs first isn't selfish – it's smart. It's about managing your energy, your resources, and your stamina so that you can show up fully for yourself, your team, your clients, and your family. If you're constantly running on empty, how will you ever be able to give your best to anyone else?

Healthy Hustle will guide you through the process of redefining success on your terms. It offers a road map for integrating smart business growth with personal wellbeing, helping you move from survival mode to a place where you can truly thrive. Whether it's through the smart growth principles that bring clarity out of chaos, the peak performance strategies that empower your team, or the time freedom models that give you back control of your life, this book provides the tools you need to build a business that doesn't just survive – but that prospers without consuming you.

But let's be clear – reading this book alone won't change your life. It's the action you take after turning the final page that will make all the difference. The concepts and tools you'll find here are your roadmap, but the journey is yours to take. Will you continue on the same path, overwhelmed and overworked? Or will you be courageous enough to do something different, to embrace the idea that you can step back, trust your team, and still see your business flourish?

The choice is yours. This book is your guide to not just surviving in business, but truly thriving in all aspects of life. As you embark on this journey, remember that the ultimate goal is not just to build a successful business, but to create a life that you love living every day. That is the essence of healthy hustle.

Janine Garner – Best-selling author, International Speaker and Business Owner

Introduction

In 2019, James B reached out looking for a different way, a better way. His business was at a growth set point. He'd grown in terms of revenue and clients, and he was feeling the pressure. It was affecting his ability to be present with his wife and young kids. He couldn't disconnect from work when he was with his family and would always have his phone within arm's reach. He was in constant demand, feeling the need to answer calls at the dinner table, always listening out for the next thing that was around the corner seeking his undivided attention.

Fast forward to today, James B recently shared with us that his business has experienced an average 98% increase in revenue year-on-year over the five years we've been working together, *with* a profit increase. Now, that's some serious growth in terms of healthy revenue and profit (particularly considering he was already an established business), and we know many business owners who wouldn't shy away from those kinds of numbers. But the revenue and profit increase weren't the most exciting part of James B's results. *They* weren't the thing we were celebrating.

There's a deeper and more meaningful aspect to why this was such a huge win. James B experienced this level of growth **and** no longer feels tethered to his business. He can leave work at work, empowering his team to step in and step up when needed. This gives him more time to go karting with his son on the weekends, pick his daughters up from school and have breakfast with his wife before work.

Now, it's likely you'll have one of three responses at this point.

1. Gasp! What does that feel like ... I want that!
2. Yeah right, there's no way that could be me. My business is different ... [insert all the reasons why it could be someone else and not you here].
3. What's the big deal? There's nothing wrong with being devoutly attached to my business and missing out on life events.

Whichever response you have, we want to remind you that achieving your next level of success is never just about external growth. It was evident from the get-go that a critical turning point for James B was the work he did on his beliefs and mindset, unlearning his old ways of working, and redefining a vision of success for himself and his family. So, when we think about thriving in business and life in the truest form, we think of James B and the positive impact these shifts in perspective and ways of working had on his business, his family, his team and his clients. You see, it's not only about the revenue results, but also about *how* you get there.

And we wonder if the fact that you've picked up this book means you see some of yourself in James B's story. Maybe you're in a similar position to where James B was?

The numbers are good, clients and sales are on the rise. Your team is growing and yet somehow you still don't feel like you're thriving. In fact, you're too busy to even think about what thriving in business could look like because you're just trying to hold it all together. You're so busy keeping all the plates spinning and trying to get off Juggle Street, yet nothing seems to work. You also don't want to risk the success of your business and how far you've come by slowing down.

Sometimes we need to slow down before we can speed up and that's why this book matters. If you want results like James B, read on.

We've written this book specifically for business owners and leaders with teams so that you can keep winning in business *and* live your best life – no more winning at all costs. You'll benefit from the combined insights and expertise of not just one but two seasoned business and leadership coaches. That's double the mix of perspectives and experience to build on your own business acumen. Having each owned successful coaching businesses, we've honed our expertise in leadership, business and sales across a variety of industries and business sizes.

What we know to be true is that there are three main reasons good folks like yourself start their businesses:*

1. To have more time with family and get free from the shackles of a day job (and a boss) ... while making good money.
2. To step into your zone of genius because you're damn good at what you do and can do it better than anyone else out there.
3. To bring a dream to life, you have a passion that became a driving force.

We'd love to know, which was it for you? Maybe it was a combination of two of these reasons? Maybe it was all the above?

If we fast forward to today, or to five, ten, twenty years down the track, the reality is often far from your dream of why you started your business in the first place. If you're like the many other business owners we work with, instead of feeling free, you feel shackled to the business. Instead of being in your genius zone, you're feeling overworked and stretched in what feels like a million different directions. And instead of spending more

---

* Note for Leaders: While you might not relate directly to the reasons someone started a business, there may be similar motivations behind why you took on a particular role or progressed in your career.

time with your family, you're spending less than when you had a day job.

The fire in your belly and the passion has diminished, and business feels chaotic. You're working beyond capacity; the hours are long, the juggle is real and sometimes you find yourself asking, is it all even worth it, because you're pulled into the whirlwind of day-to-day craziness, delivering for clients, creating an amazing environment for your team, keeping the business afloat, all while dealing with the many other aspects of life that are thrown at you. With all this going on, it's no wonder there's a growing chasm between *why* you went into business and the *current reality* of your day-to-day life in business.

But you know how this story goes. You get up, and you keep hustling ... harder.

There's no doubt about it, you've reached a level of success that many would envy. You unequivocally and totally rock! You've beat the statistics, the naysayers and the tumultuous times in business. And we are in awe of your tenacity, determination and resilience. You had to hustle hard, and it worked. The business grew, the team grew, and you found yourself celebrating successes along the way.

But at what cost?

The hardcore (old-school) 'hustle for success' formula has created a conundrum that you're most likely dealing with today. And it's this: You've been doing things this way for so long you have plenty of evidence to show that your business will grow *if* you hustle, stay in the minutiae and do it all yourself. This has now become a subconscious belief that's been created and proven time and time again with every day, month, year you've been in business. This belief of 'hustle hard at all costs', 'do it all', 'don't stop' way of working has become a driving force (and arguably the price of) your success. Do you know how to do business any other way?

Here's our first truth bomb: What got you to this level of success is not going to be what gets you to your next frontier of growth.

We wrote this book to help you unlearn, and relearn, healthy hustle strategies for where you are right now. To show you there is a better way so that you can get control back of your destiny and no longer let your business control your life. To start a conversation about the limits and boundaries of hustle. So, what is healthy hustle?

In our world, healthy hustle is ...

- Being driven, tenacious, determined but **not** at all costs.
- Prioritising life, just as much as business.
- Releasing the weight of expectation of how we *should* do business.
- Winning in both business, and life.

Ultimately healthy hustle is the balance of knowing when to push and when to pull back. It's success without health issues from stress. It's achieving goals without sacrificing time doing things we enjoy.

It's time for you to redefine success in a way that fits you and your lifestyle. We're not here to tell you what healthy hustle is for you. You need to decide that. We're here to inspire and challenge your thinking around what it could be for you. Our definition could be different to yours. And that's okay!

You might bristle at the word hustle. You might be thinking 'why hustle at all?'

The answer is because we need the hustle. Just like we need stress, positive stress, to thrive (more about this further along in the book). The upside of hustle is that it can create momentum, action, energy, focus and drive. The problem is, we've taken it too far.

There's no one size fits all in business. If the years post-Covid have taught us anything, it's this. It might seem like the easy option to continue as is, not challenge the status quo. But – as you'll learn through understanding the phases of smart business growth and the other insights and frameworks in this book – if you don't do anything, your business will either plateau or be at risk of decline.

The **7 Business Truths** we must embrace for healthy hustle:

1. You can have a super successful business while still having a life.
2. You've been sold a lie that the only way to keep succeeding is to 'work harder'.
3. Burnout and being busy are not badges of honour.
4. Business can grow without subscribing to the push, stress, hard hustle culture.
5. It's up to you to break the rules of business that don't work for you.
6. You don't have to be tethered to your business to thrive in business.
7. You can create a thriving business on your own terms.

The road map to embrace smart business growth, leverage leadership for peak performance and get back time freedom are laid out in the following pages. We're giving you the blueprint and real-life reference points as your road map.

Here's our promise: We've got you! If we need to believe in these truths for you until you believe them for yourself, then that's what we'll do. Our hope is that by the time you've finished reading this book, you'll see all these 7 Business Truths as your reality.

Here's our ask: Be open-minded and give it a go. Park any 'why it won't work' reasons that come up and instead try to focus on the question 'how could this work?'. This is about expanding your thinking and exploring what could be.

We've had a lot of tough conversations with business owners over the years and have identified the patterns that make a successful, sustainable business and those that cause businesses to fail, or business owners to burnout. Which, of course, has a ripple effect on all those around them. We've both worked in leadership roles in corporate, big business environments and have also learnt the agile ways of working in small businesses. The powerful combination of these two perspectives is weaved throughout this book, and all the work we do.

We're obsessed with contributing to a new era of business and leadership that values humanness, champions smart growth, and cultivates a culture of healthy hustle to redefine success and magnify our impact on people.

This book is broken into three parts:

1. How Did We Get Here?
2. How Do We Get There?
3. The Road Ahead.

Woven throughout are real-life stories of people in our community who we've worked with either as clients or interviewed on our podcast. They're creating phenomenal change in their businesses so that they, their teams *and* their businesses can thrive well into the future.

At the back of the book, you'll see we've created a Choose Your Own Adventure Map of the exercises and key frameworks we take you through. There's also dedicated space for you to make notes so that you can create your own cheat sheet to come back to whenever you need.

We've also designed the book for you to be able to open to any chapter and find something that can immediately be applied to your business. If you have a particular area you want to start working on, follow the guide below.

- **Business planning**

  Chapter 3. Smart Growth: Chaos to Clarity

- **Sales**

  Bonus section of Chapter 3: Let's Talk Sales

- **Team development**

  Chapter 4. Peak Performance: Stepping Off Juggle Street

- **Time management**

  Chapter 5. Time Freedom: Your Path to Time Freedom

- **Identifying what phase of smart growth you're in**

  Chapter 6. Your Smart Growth Blueprint

Or, of course, you can read along chapter by chapter.

If you were a kid in the 1980s, you might remember the *Choose Your Own Adventure* books. They were filled to the brim with different journeys and escapades, roadblocks and obstacles to overcome, as well as triumphs and celebrations of milestones. As the reader, you were the star of the show. You could be a daring spy, a fearless mountain climber, or a brilliant detective. There were unexpected twists, trick endings and you couldn't backtrack to the exact same spot where you started if you regretted your decision. The stakes were high, and they certainly felt real. Just like in business.

At various points in the *Choose Your Own Adventure* books, you could choose where to go next. There could be an option taking you down the seemingly treacherous yet feasibly lucrative path, it feels a bit risky and daring but it could be worth the risk. Or there could be an option that feels a little safer, more familiar and predictable, but you never really knew if it was the safe option until you got to the end.

We want you to think of this book as your own 'Choose Your Own Adventure' story. Right now, in this very moment, you have three options laid out in front of you. Which will you choose?

Path 1. Keep going as you are. Maintaining your existing strategies and methods as challenges pop up. Whilst you know there could be a better way, you're not ready to veer away from the status quo (or current state of 'hustle').

Path 2. Bury your head in the sand. Avoiding challenges and refusing to acknowledge issues hoping they'll resolve themselves. Ignoring problems and wishing they'll go away.

Path 3. Be courageous enough to do things differently. Trying new approaches, expanding comfort zones and challenging the norm. Finding new ways to reach new heights in business.

Each decision you make as a leader takes you down a different path with its own set of challenges and potential rewards. Some paths feel scarier than others. Some feel safer but it could be a trick to keep you in your comfort zone. And staying in your comfort zone will eventually become uncomfortable. As one of our favourite mentors, Joe Pane says, "everything in the universe without exception is expanding or shrinking, breathing out or breathing in, green and growing or ripe and rotting." So, which will it be?

This is an invitation for you to join us if you want to take Path 3.

HEALTHY HUSTLE

PART ONE.

How Did We Get Here?

It's time to define what hustle and healthy hustle is (and isn't) in your world view, and how it's affecting both you personally and your business results. What are the negative side effects to the old-school hustle that's become such a prevalent part of society and, equally, how could healthy hustle serve you better?

The sad truth is that the longer you're in business, the more the stats are against you. When you know what the common reasons for business failure are, you can arm yourself and be ready for the battle. Or hopefully avoid the battle all together. There are things in your business you might be ignoring, and they could be the things that are going to get you to smart growth. What are they and why do they matter?

There's a typical pain point in businesses on the trajectory of time and results that becomes a potential growth point to move the business forward. You can either grow or stay the same, wish and hope for growth, or go into denial and risk decline.

Being aware of this pain point gives you the opportunity to break the cycles that are unhelpful for your business and your team. When we know better, we do better. And honestly, it's our responsibility to step up and grow smartly, not through hard relentless hustle. Because, as Marshall Goldsmith so famously said, "What got you here won't get you there" ... which in this context is your next horizon. Your next evolution.

Of course, you can always keep going as is, and ignore that niggling feeling that there could be a better, different way of working and growing your business (that doesn't involve you being so relied on in the day-to-day operations). But we hope you choose to get curious and explore our ideas about leaning into a healthier hustle, get inspired by the stories of business leaders who have been where you are now, and have a go at using the practical tools and exercises shared in the following pages.

CHAPTER ONE.

The Hours are Long: The Juggle is Real

LET'S TALK ABOUT THE HUSTLE

For the last decade, we've been slightly obsessed with this idea of 'hustle'. What it means, the impact on us as humans and the flow-on effect to our businesses, families and lives.

Even in the early days of business, we absolutely loved bringing the conversation of understanding hustle to the table. Always curious to find out what 'hustle' meant to the high-performing business leaders we worked with, and often asking the question, "What does hustle mean to you?" We wonder, how would you answer that question today?

We found it fascinating that very rarely did two people answer in the exact same way. Some people said hustle is conning people or ripping people off. Others said they think of it as hard work, tenacity and kicking goals. We think the strangest answer was 'a dance' (if you don't know it, apparently it was all the rage in the 1970s). And there's also a movie out there called *The Hustler* ... go figure.

If we look up the *Oxford Dictionary* definition of hustle, we'll find:

> Push roughly; jostle.
>
> Obtain illicitly or by forceful action.
>
> A state of great activity.
>
> A fraud or swindle.

Or if we check out the *Urban Dictionary*:*

> To strive headstrong and voraciously towards a goal.
>
> To seek out and acquire sums of money, preferably large sums, often by unscrupulous means.

So, whose meaning, and definition of hustle is correct?

Well, yours is. Ours is. Theirs is. We're all right!

---

* Urban Dictionary is a crowdsourced English-language online dictionary for slang words and phrases.

Because nothing has meaning except the meaning we give it. And the meaning we give words happens subconsciously based on our values and our experiences. Experiences like doing the dance in the 1970s, watching a movie called *The Hustler*, or being ripped off and pushed into buying something and feeling like we've been swindled. All these are experiences and events that shape what we believe to be true. They attach the meaning that we apply to words.

Perception is reality *regardless* of what the dictionary definition is.

Personally, for me (Nicky), my relationship with hustle has changed over time. In the early days I hustled my way to success in my corporate and business career. Having grown up in housing commission, I had a real drive to succeed, to make money and have as many experiences as I could along the way. I did my best to fit as much as possible into this wild ride of life. I remember a mentor when I was in my early twenties warning me about this concept of burning the candle at both ends. Hah! But I had something to prove and apparently I was invincible.

So, as I got older, I continued to work my butt off, putting in the long hours, not stopping and trying to do it all. I took pride in being the last one in the office. I was all things to all people and eventually it led me to burnout where I felt trapped with a body, mind and energy that were unrecognisable to me. Yet, even after burnout (not a pleasant experience to say the least), I *still* found myself deeply wound up in the cycle of hustle, push culture.

The result?

Career progression, a successful and growing business, revenue and profit I'd once only dreamed of. This is the side of success people could see. What they didn't see was the panic attack that landed me in ER, the pneumonia from pushing too hard when I was sick, finding myself lying Elizabeth Gilbert-style (oh yes, *Eat*

Pray Love) on the floor completely overwhelmed. And these are things that happened *after* my first experience of burnout.

After embracing (and, let's be honest, celebrating) the hardcore nature of old-school hustle till I drop, it got me thinking: There must be a better way! This can't be what success looks like. Feeling exhausted, running to the finish line at the end of each year or the end of the week ... or even the end of each day.

Now there's nothing wrong with being driven and an action-taker – in fact it's needed. And we don't know about you, but it's how we're wired and we don't want that to change. However, when it comes to hustle culture, there's a winning-at-all-costs mentality that seems to take over. There's a lie we're being told that we need to be constantly 'on' and if we're not, we're wasting time. That to stop, means being lazy or inefficient. Think about it, even elite athletes need time to pause and recover.

Imagine you're an elite athlete and your area of sport is business (or leadership). How are you taking care of your body, your mind and your energy to make sure you keep performing at your best?

The key is to find the sweet spot between taking enough action and go-getting to move forward at a steady pace, but not so much that it becomes all-consuming and sucks the life out of you. This sweet spot is *healthy hustle*.

STUCK IN THE WHIRLWIND

In business we want to be like the best athlete, to go from strength to strength. We're in this business where it's a game of inches. Incremental growth and the 1% can sometimes be more powerful than 100%. Because it's not *just* about getting better and better or doing more and more each day. It's also about enjoying the process – that can be fulfilling on its own.

You've heard the saying, it's not about the destination, it's about the journey. Well, we want to question, why can't it be both?

Why can't it be about the destination *and* the journey!

Right now, businesses are stuck in a whirlwind. They are in chaos, with many business owners and leaders feeling like they are living every day on Juggle Street. We're living in a culture that has us addicted to and always wanting 'more'. This feeling of chaos is presenting itself in so many ways with many people already at risk of burnout. According to a Deloitte survey in 2018, 77% of employees reported experiencing burnout in their current job. As a collective, we're exhausted. Mental health issues are going through the roof. Kids are struggling. Parents are struggling. The same Deloitte survey stated 91% of people say having an unmanageable amount of stress or frustration negatively impacts the quality of their work. Team engagement is dropping, staff turnover is at an all-time high. According to Gallup, burned-out employees are 2.6 times as likely to be actively seeking a different job.

There's panic about the future of work and a scramble to find the next big thing. All you need to do is turn on any media channel and you can feel the chaos. We've gotten ourselves so tangled in the web of fast-paced action and too many options (seriously – does anyone else have decision fatigue about what to watch on all the streaming channels or is it just us?) that we can't see the forest for the trees. We're stuck in a busy trap.

To overcome the chaos, maybe you've invested in growing your team, hoping it would give you capacity to get more stuff done but instead you still feel like there's even more balls in the air. Many hands make light work, don't they? Isn't that what they say? What they don't tell you is that along with those many hands come many different opinions, mindsets, ways of thinking, ways of doing. And so, a part of the journey to move from Juggle Street to peak performance is not always simple because people are complex. Yet the way we lead them doesn't have to be.

And let's not forget the sales pressure – while your lead generation might be on fire, your internal sales systems could be letting you down. Sales growth in the business might still be solely reliant on you, and you know you need to empower and train your team, but you don't have the time to even think about transferring the knowledge from your head into a development plan or coaching for your team members.

Ultimately, what we want is for you to be able to leverage smart growth, have your team performing optimally and for everyone in the business to enjoy time freedom. There's a calling for a gentler way, a slower pace, the option of choice. We can see it in the slow living movement that came about from a yearning to live a more balanced, present and meaningful life. The slow living movement is a lifestyle that encourages a slower approach to aspects of everyday life, including completing tasks at a leisurely pace.

And yet, we get it, you don't want to risk the success you've already achieved by slowing down. Trust us, we know what it's like to be at the point of wanting a better way, and at the same time concerned about risking it all by stopping or doing things differently. Because there are still goals to chase down and there's a fun aspect to the fast side of living that maybe you're not ready to give up just yet (or ever).

THE STATS ARE AGAINST US

We're sure you've heard stats for early days in business (in case you haven't, 60% of businesses will fail within the first three years), but did you know the longer you're in business, the more the stats are against you?

Research shows that 80% of businesses will fail within twenty years. Our jaws dropped when we first heard this stat. There's so much focus on getting through the early years of business but what about the established businesses that have been around the block a few times. They've got the war wounds to show from turbulent times. The trophies in the poolroom from their glory days. And apparently, they're not out of the woods despite the many years of doing their thing!

As we delve a little deeper, we uncover three main reasons (outside of poor cashflow management) that businesses fail:

- Lack of staff training.
- No strategy.
- Business owners getting stuck in day-to-day operations.

Do any of these reasons surprise you? What we find most heartening is that every single one is within your control. With the right blueprint and knowing where to focus your and your team's attention, you can futureproof your business and steer clear of becoming yet another statistic.

Here's our caution sign: If you don't address these potential pitfalls, you could wind up being another statistic. You already could be on the path to resenting your business, hitting the burnout wall and deciding to walk away from your business entirely. Now's the time to pump the brakes and pause.

Let's take a moment.

ACTION WITH PURPOSE

Rate yourself from 1 to 10 in each of these areas, where 1 means there's nothing in place in this area and 10 means not only is it happening, but it's also happening consistently.

Be brutally honest with where you sit as you read through each point.

1. Consistent staff training and upskilling.
   YOUR SCORE __ /10

Is there consistent training and upskilling of all staff, not only in their area of responsibility, expertise and product knowledge but also in areas of professional development like adapting to change, tapping into a high-performance mindset, resilience?

2. Business strategy in place.
   YOUR SCORE __ /10

Do you have a business strategy to guide you and the team to where you want to take the business? Einstein said, "Everything should be made as simple as possible, but no simpler." We say, "Business planning should

be made as simple as possible, but no simpler." This means that there must be enough juice in your plan to make the squeeze meaningful and last the distance, but not so much that it's overflowing and becomes too much to keep track of.

3. Business owners and leaders **don't** get caught up in the day-to-day whirlwind of the business. YOUR SCORE __ /10

Oof! We know you feel this, and you feel it deeply. You're not getting pulled into the whirlwind or the busy trap. You can take time away from the office without being constantly connected to devices and the team makes autonomous decisions on your behalf. You're not dealing with client calls on the weekends.

Check out your results. What did you get out of 30? Is there a pattern in your scores, specific areas that surprise you by being low or high? If your scores are on the lower side, we've got you! In the pages that follow, we're giving you the blueprint to continue to build a sustainable business.

LET'S GET REAL

In my house we have what we call a doom room (if you're also in a neurospicy household, you might relate). It's the room in the house where things get dumped, sometimes never to return. Can you relate to any of these:

- Someone's coming over and you have to tidy up real quick, put it in the doom room.
- Don't have time to put away the washing before the cleaner gets here, pop it in the doom room.
- Something doesn't have its own place and you're sick of seeing it, to the doom room!

You get the picture. Not to air my dirty laundry for everyone to see, but when I think about this idea of a doom room, I wonder, *What's in the metaphorical doom room of your business?*

It's likely to be the things you already have on your radar that:

- Need your attention but maybe are not the sexiest or most fun tasks so it's easier to ignore (hello cashflow planning and profit management or sales systems).
- You must do but you don't have time (like coaching and training your team).
- Are important but they're not urgent so they can wait (we're looking at you processes and documentation).

If there's any chance of breaking out of the day-to-day whirlwind, opening the door to your doom room and shining the light in is the only way. The best way to do this? Getting good at smart business growth.

Okay, okay, you've heard us go on and on about smart business growth, heck it's plastered all over our website, socials, it's the name of our podcast and we'll talk about it at any chance we get. Let us take you through exactly what smart business growth means. There are three key areas that need to be in place to classify business growth as smart growth.

1. An *intentional* approach to planning, sales and profit.

What this looks like:

- Challenging the norms around what business success looks like for you.
- Having sales *and* profit targets (a $10 million dollar turnover means nothing if you're not making a profit. Profit gives you freedom and choice, and allows you to enjoy the rewards of all your work).
- Including a section in your business plan that's dedicated to life goals. This gives you a holistic approach to reach your 'true north' in all areas of business and life, and fosters optimal energy and an environment for sustainable success.

2. Building an empowered and autonomous team.

What this looks like:

- Making sure both your business and your team are growing and striving for peak performance.
- Having a clear definition of high performance that becomes the compass of behaviour and values guiding the team's actions.
- Establishing consistent operating rhythms that create a culture of transparency to allow you to trust in the team stepping up so you can take a step back.

3. Establishing time freedom as a standard, for *all* people in the business.

What this looks like:

- Leveraging natural drivers and strengths of people to maximise return on effort, reducing number of hours worked, and shifting the focus away from time and towards outcomes.

- Being crystal clear on priorities to create a proactive environment instead of a rushed and reactive environment.
- Establishing solid boundaries and unspoken ground rules that apply for all in the business ... even (especially) you!

Business owners and leaders often admit to being the bottleneck in their own business. It comes down to feeling like there's no time, or not knowing where to start that stops them from doing things a different way from how they've always done it.

Good is the barrier to challenging the status quo because good is comfortable. It takes more gusto to create change when things are good, and the pay-off when you do is that it will take things *from* good *to* great.

IT'S OUR DUTY OF CARE

The four-hour work week might be a myth when you're starting out in business, but what if it could be a reality for you now? In the early days, you needed to put in **double the effort for half the reward**. Now it's time for you to get **double the result with half the effort**. You've earned your stripes in terms of time in business, size of your team, your business model and how you serve your clients. Maybe it's time to challenge the conventional thinking of what a successful business looks like. Dare to dream and think differently.

What if the opposite of what you believe a 'successful business' looks like could be true? If the 5 am Club didn't have to be the only way to start your morning in a 'successful' way. If you could achieve massive results without a massive team. Or if you could do more by doing less. We're not here to say what definition of success is right or wrong for you. That's up to you to figure out. What we do want to do is get you to think deliberately about what a great business by design looks like for you! We want to challenge your thinking around the status quo and the 'norms' that have automatically been set for you. Have you thinking outside the box about what your business could be like. A great way to get into creative thinking is by looking at what your *outrageous opposites* could be. Let's get curious and map it out.

Imagine you have a magic wand in your hand and anything could be true. There's no right or wrong and the limitations of the stories you tell yourself don't exist right now. Park them and put them to the side if they come up (you can always pick them up later).

Write a list of what success looks like to you right now – whether you do them or not doesn't matter. This is a list of things you *believe* to be true about a successful businessperson, CEO, founder, director, manager.

To help kick you off, things that could be on the list (these are just a guide to get you started, make sure you write your own ideas) are:

- 5 am Club.
- Starting work at 8 am.
- Working after hours.
- Working long hours (70+ hours a week), six or seven days a week.
- Having a team of 50+ full-time workers in an office.
- $10 million+ turnover.
- Having a bricks and mortar office.

- On the go constantly, busy, busy ...
  shows importance.
- Knowing the detail of all clients and attending
  every client meeting.
- Being across all detail in the business, across
  all departments.

Now get playful and bring your 'what ifs' to the party. Write down what *could be* the outrageous opposite of each item on your list?

Note: It's important to park any doubts around how these things are achievable, that comes later. Remember, right now you have a magic wand in your hand:

- Sleeping until 8 am.
- Starting work at 10 am.
- Finishing at 5 pm.
- Working three days a week, four hours a day.
- Having a team of 20 achieving results and a
  flexible workforce.
- $5 million turnover – with MORE profit!
- Moving to online or a flexible
  working environment.
- Enjoying space to do nothing, actual gaps in
  the calendar.
- Only knowing the need-to-knows and tapping
  into your team who are across important details.

- Trusting your inner circle of leaders to have things under control.

When you have your list of outrageous opposites, you can start to observe, ideate, get curious about how they could become your reality. What if it is your reality? What would change for you if you eased the pressure of how it *should* be and focused instead on how you *want* it to be? No rules, no bad ideas, just getting creative with ideas **and** creative with how you could achieve it.

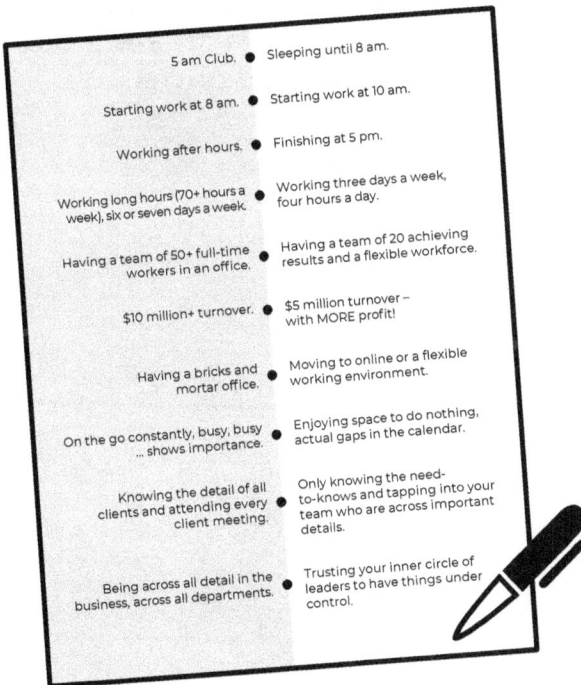

5 am Club.	Sleeping until 8 am.
Starting work at 8 am.	Starting work at 10 am.
Working after hours.	Finishing at 5 pm.
Working long hours (70+ hours a week), six or seven days a week.	Working three days a week, four hours a day.
Having a team of 50+ full-time workers in an office.	Having a team of 20 achieving results and a flexible workforce.
$10 million+ turnover.	$5 million turnover – with MORE profit!
Having a bricks and mortar office.	Moving to online or a flexible working environment.
On the go constantly, busy, busy ... shows importance.	Enjoying space to do nothing, actual gaps in the calendar.
Knowing the detail of all clients and attending every client meeting.	Only knowing the need-to-knows and tapping into your team who are across important details.
Being across all detail in the business, across all departments.	Trusting your inner circle of leaders to have things under control.

Past success doesn't guarantee future success and continuing to only use the same approach you have previously is fraught with danger. Hustle culture is out of control and if you can take stock of where you sit on the hustle spectrum (unhealthy or healthy), it will give you the chance to gain some control over the shifting sands that are creating your ideal (or not ideal) future in business.

It's our responsibility as a collective to lead the charge when it comes to growing our businesses in a balanced way and show that winning doesn't have to be at a cost, or a sacrifice of joy and life. Let us ask you, if not now, then when? If not you, then who? The impact of creating change on you, your family, your team, your business and the flow-on effect to your community is huge (and something to embrace). In the words of Julia Roberts in Pretty Woman, not doing anything is a "Big mistake. Big. Huge."

It's time to release the weight of expectations on how you *should* be doing business, so that you can create a business on your own terms.

The Daily Grind

Caitlin was three years into her business, a HR firm started in the thick of Covid crazy, when she made the decision to prioritise a pause and join a session we ran called How to Thrive in Business ... Without the Burnout.

A week later, we received a voice message from Caitlin. One of the 1% actions she took from that day was to book a long-overdue doctor's appointment as she'd been noticing a 'weird pain' in her jaw.

They found a hairline fracture in her bottom jaw caused by grinding her teeth.

Can you imagine continuing with the pain of a hairline fracture because you're so entrenched in the daily grind and don't have time to get it checked out. Not to mention the amount of stress that would cause that amount of grinding! You might have had a similar experience yourself. In fact, you most likely have but possibly haven't taken the time to acknowledge the significant reality that this has become your norm.

Caitlin told us after the workshop that she was stuck in survival mode despite doing all the courses, training and personal development. Caitlin is an incredibly smart and savvy businesswoman doing many wonderful things, not only in her business but also in her community. She is a giver in every sense of the word. The obvious that screams out here is that she was giving to everyone around her, putting herself last. And in her words, this was the kick up the backside she knew she needed.

The duty of care Caitlin has to take care of herself isn't just for her. It's for all the people around her that she works with and impacts every day, as well as her team, her family, and her community organisations that she gives so generously to. Being stuck in the whirlwind can be a blocker to the most foundational levels of self-care – like going to a doctor.

Taking the 1% action, in this case coming along to our workshop and doing the one action she committed to, was the first step to her no longer avoiding what she knew needed attention. For Caitlin, it wasn't her business tasks that were locked away in a doom room but those related to her health and wellbeing.

Is your business more important than your health sometimes? Are you waiting to stumble on major health issues by chance because you're burying your head in the sand, don't have time or it's not the most important thing on your list right now rather than proactively preventing them?

THE HOURS ARE LONG: THE JUGGLE IS REAL

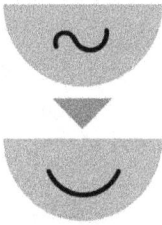

CHAPTER TWO.

Hustle to Happy

GET A LIFE

We'll never forget the first conversation we had with James B. He said, "I just want to be able to take a holiday without being needed by work. Without being contacted by my team or clients and to be able to completely switch off!' In essence, what he was saying was, "I want my life back."

When we talk to live audiences about this idea of getting a life, and having holidays where you're uncontactable, there's always an awkward rumble of laughter. I mean, the thought of having a proper holiday, how great would that be right?!

The fact that it is such a common predicament among business owners to not have a proper holiday shouldn't be something that makes us awkwardly laugh. It's a serious state of affairs and we need to create change.

Research reveals that in Australia only **43% of small business owners take at least four weeks** of leave annually. A little over **25% take two weeks or less** each year, and **14% don't even remember** the last time they had a holiday! Where do you sit?

We know that when small business owners and leaders do take leave, many find it hard to detach from the business. Are you one of the 77% of people who still think about your business when on holidays?

Quick question: Do you make sure your team takes their annual leave? If yes, then why not you?

Hold up! Before you get your phone out to send us an email listing all the reasons why it's different for you and why you can't take holidays where you can completely switch off, let's sit on this for a minute.

We all know the logical upside to taking holidays. Increase in productivity, decrease in sick leave, higher engagement. There's also the fact that it makes you a happier, more whole and less cranky human (which is great for everyone).

But you already know this because as business owners, CEOs, leaders, it's why you make sure your team members take proper holidays. Not taking leave impacts the bottom line and creates cashflow risk, as well as impacting the emotional capacity and efficiency of your people. It's Business 101.

So why is it different for you? Those benefits still apply to you, don't they? There isn't a superhuman energy source that's been discovered as far as we're aware that makes you immune, and yet, the stats show that most of you are not playing by the same rules when it comes to taking proper breaks.

UNLEARNING WAYS OF WORKING

The beliefs that drive your individual ways of working have an impact not only on you as an individual and on your family, but also on your team members, their families, your community and society at large.

There's a freedom that comes with not feeling chained to your business, and breaking away from the belief that success only happens when knee-deep in and hustling hard. You get to enjoy the space that comes with being able to choose where you spend your time and the grace of being present in many of life's moments – when you usually wouldn't.

Taking a pause and seeking out a better and different way allows us to reflect internally and explore what's driving our view of success. Where did it come from and is it *our* truth or someone else's that has been imprinted into our map of the world, or in other words how we see and experience the world.

It's time for you, as a business owner and leader, to have autonomy over your business and break the cycles you don't yet realise are holding you back. It's time to wake up from the dream state you've been in for too long, to stop taking on other world views without the critical thinking to realise if it is truly how you see success. And if you're already doing this – bravo!

We live in a very push, go-go-go till we drop culture. Busy is a badge of honour and burnout is just another b-word keeping us trapped. Data from Roy Morgan showed heading into the 2023/24 summer break, over 8.8 million Australians in paid employment had 200 million days of annual leave due – up from 185 million days two years earlier.

There's a disturbing trend called leavism, first identified by Professor Cary Cooper and his colleagues at Manchester University in 2014. This is where people work on their holidays or when they're unwell (sound familiar?). Online lender OnDeck Australia research backs this up. They found 77% of small business owners still think about their business when on holiday, and one in five would check in with the business regularly while on leave.

We've got to start thinking differently about how connected we need to be to our business for it to grow and thrive; for our teams to grow and thrive. This is the only way true, lasting change can happen. But this change doesn't happen when you and your teams are exhausted and pushing through when you're sick or meant to be switched off and relaxing. Just imagine if you could still grow your business, kick those big, hairy audacious goals, be super freaking successful AND if you could do it smarter and not harder.

Working smart not hard is about unlearning the ways of working that have gone before us. When we entered the Industrial Revolution during the late 1700s to early 1800s, the pace of work became faster and faster. Work was performed in factories built to house machines and workers were forced to work very long hours to keep those machines operating, up to sixteen hours a day, six days per week.

THE TIPPING POINT

Fast forward 200 years and the expectations of our modern ways of working have seemingly changed. We say seemingly because, yes, we now have so many more options and choices on where and how to work (particularly with hybrid and remote working these days). We're no longer restricted to factory work or being forced to work ninety-six hours a week, and yet, there's still a crazy amount of pressure business leaders put on themselves (and their teams*) around the big hours they're working.

Pushing through and working long hours is not good for business. There may be more to this than you realise. When it comes to productivity, there's a tipping point when work becomes less effective. Anything beyond fifty hours in a week and you're literally wasting your time.

A study by Stanford University Economics Professor John Pencavel found that productivity declines sharply when a person works more than fifty hours a week.

After fifty hours, productivity drops so much that putting in more hours is pointless. Those working seventy hours a week get the same amount of work done as someone working fifty hours a week.

That's twenty hours a week that could be spent sleeping, having fun, doing your favourite hobby, chilling out, being with your favourite humans (or pets). What would you do with an extra twenty hours a week? Take a moment to answer that question. To really think on it and plan exactly what you would do with this extra time.

---

* Even if you're not explicitly telling your team to work longer hours, they're observing your behaviours!

Imagine what it would be like if you could get your life back. What would you do with more time? Where would you spend it and who would you spend it with? Remember the magic wand you had for the outrageous opposites exercise? Now that you have the extra time, what will you do with it?

GROWTH VS. INERTIA – THE SILENT KILLER OF BUSINESS

There's a growth set point in every business. In fact, there'll be many over the lifespan of a business. It's a point of inflection for either perturbation and pain or growth and potential. It's the point James B was at when he came to us and it's the typical trajectory for any successful business factoring in results over time as you can see in figure 1.

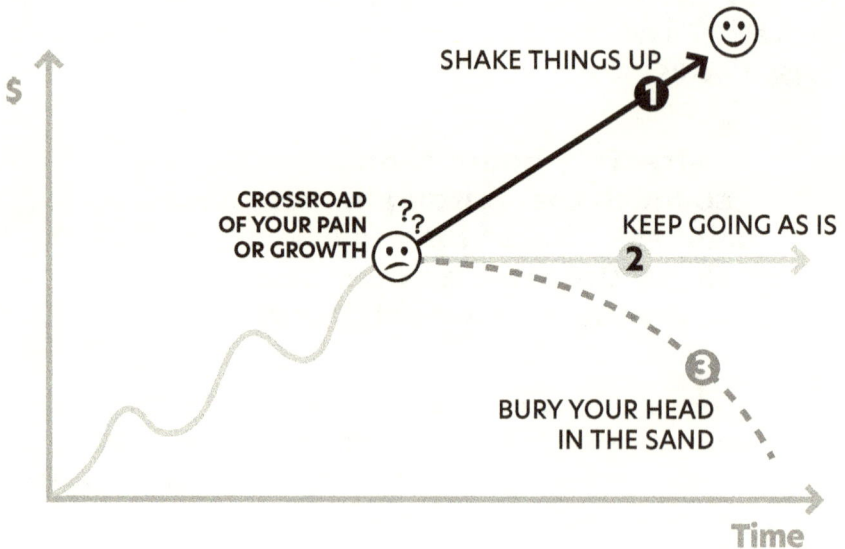

$

SHAKE THINGS UP ➊

CROSSROAD OF YOUR PAIN OR GROWTH ??

KEEP GOING AS IS ➋

➌ BURY YOUR HEAD IN THE SAND

Time

Figure 1

When you're at the crossroad of your pain or growth set point, it feels uncomfortable. It's uneasy and it doesn't feel great. And yet it's also a significant point of growth potential, that if you choose to lean into the discomfort, you'll reap the inevitable and bountiful rewards of doing so.

The growth set point is the take off point for your next frontier of growth. It's the pivotal moment where results can be exponentially accelerated beyond where you are now.

To hit this crossroad, you had to have experienced existing growth in your business. There's been a level of success, sales are flowing, the team continues to grow, sometimes the business grows too quickly and the systems, structure, and upskilling can't keep up.

And as the business owner, you start to question what your 'next' looks like. You're getting pulled into the whirlwind of the day-to-day and while there's been good results to date, you can feel a shift in the air. Change is afoot.

As you can see in the graph, you have an option to shake things up (marked 1 in Figure 1) in a way that embraces smart growth, encourages people leadership and embeds peak performance principles. You could reflect on what has worked to date, what to keep and replicate and, just as importantly, what to let go of. You could also foster adaptability and innovation in the ways of working, allowing the business to thrive, evolve and keep pace with the world around you. Creating an environment conducive to continuous improvement and long-term success not only ensures the continued growth of your business but also enables you to gradually step back. This helps you build confidence and strength in the capabilities of your team and the processes in your business. This is a proactive stance that positions your business to be around for another twenty years, and to become a vehicle for you to live your best life, instead of being the thing that keeps you stuck in the busy trap.

Alternatively, you can continue as is (marked 2 in Figure 1). Maybe you'll get halfway through this book, maybe you'll finish it or stick it on a bookshelf never to be seen again. If nothing changes, nothing changes. Except it does. You'll notice the business will plateau and what was once a focus on high performance and results will gradually fade into complacency. A sense of stagnation and inertia will overtake the drive for excellence previously felt and apathy will override giving a slow death to the passion you once had. Of course, this will have a flow-on effect to your team members, your clients and how you show up for them. The momentum you once had (that you may still have right now) will eventually dwindle.

Or perhaps you'll subconsciously decide to bury your head in the sand (marked 3 in Figure 1). Avoid the telltale signs, ignore that niggling feeling that things could be better, and hope that issues will resolve themselves. Yet, as time goes on, your commitment and engagement in the business is fractured. The care factor declines, and this might take a personal toll getting you on the way to, if not hitting, a burnout wall. You could find yourself resenting the very business and dream you once poured your heart and soul into, or worse, contemplating walking away altogether. Meanwhile, your team will sense the disengagement and lack of direction, hugely impacting morale and productivity. Without a thriving culture of active engagement, transparency and purpose, your team will feel bored and undervalued. Your business becomes vulnerable to high attrition rates, further impacting people and culture. You can see where this leads, the impact on clients, the impact to your ever-increasing workload, the impact on you and those who matter the most.

Remember when we gave you three paths to choose from in this Choose Your Own Adventure? The time has come. If you choose the path of courage to do things differently, then you're in the right place because "what got you here won't get you there."

GROW SMART NOT HARD

There's a reason you picked up this book. What was it? The promise of a healthier way to hustle. The idea of leveraging peak performance within your team. Or perhaps it was the idea that growth can be smart, not hard. Whichever it was, the ideas and principles in this book are just theory if you choose the path of avoidance or apathy.

We're not here to tell you how to run your business. You know your business better than anyone and you've been doing this gig for a while. What we are here to do is to challenge your way of thinking. To break the mould of what success looks like, make it better and expand on what you've already got going on. We're here to have a conversation with you about what really matters when it comes to outcomes in business and to provide you with some different perspectives to try on and see how they fit.

It's time we started thinking differently about business growth. It's time we get deeper into the nuts and bolts around the purpose of your business.

Not from a marketing standpoint, but from a YOU standpoint.

The only way you can create sustainable growth is to redefine the status quo. You're a genius in your area of expertise. You've got to be doing something right to get this far. So, this framework that we're taking you through is not about changing everything. Or about change for the sake of it. It's about filtering what you already have through what you want in the future.

If you decide to put in place the systems and frameworks to move beyond the pain of discomfort and the unknown, and embrace the growth set point, the impact on your culture and people will lead you to your success point. We promise, you can move away from unresourceful chaos (and embrace a more resourceful beautiful chaos) to embed smart growth.

Fundamentally unlearning *some* of your ways of working (there's a heck of a lot in there we want to keep), choosing what path you'll take and having a reality check will give you the time and capacity to think, to ideate, to connect and take your business to its full potential.

And when you do that, your business is strong, your team is strong, and you can finally start living and breathing the life you want. No more feeling tethered and chained to the business, or feeling like you have one foot in all areas of life without ever being fully in one. Your loved ones will be happy to have you back and your business will thrive with empowered staff and satisfied clients.

Take a moment to remember the reasons why you went into business. Reconnect and reflect on the following questions:

+ **Why did you start your business?**

+ **Has that reason changed for you now?**

+ **Are you achieving this reason: such as lifestyle, time with loved ones, making an impact?**

    • If no, why?

    • If yes, acknowledge the awesomeness of that. Then ask how could it be even better?

+ **Consider, how big is the gap between your dream and current reality?**

    • How serious are you about closing the gap?

Smart growth is the way. And you're not alone in this adventure, it's time for you to choose your next chapter!

I Would've Walked Away

When we met Jodie, she was at a significant pain point and her business was in chaos. Jodie and her mum had run the business together for twenty-five years, but when her mum got sick, Jodie was left to run the business herself with twenty-five staff and an overflowing book of clients (including hefty waiting lists). It's fair to say she was overwhelmed juggling the day-to-day operations and the administration requirements. She was trying to find her feet and work out how to keep the business moving forward in a positive manner. All the while struggling to fend off the feeling of burnout that was building with every long day and weekend she was working.

Jodie was craving certainty. She needed guidance and direction on the best way to work smart, not hard. She was grappling with the possibility that if her mum didn't come back to work, she'd be left to manage the business by herself. Without the systems in place and a plan to make it all happen, she was desperate for a support structure on how best to move forward.

After eight months of unlearning some of her previous ways of working, Jodie noticed she was seeing things differently than she would've in the past. She found herself challenging her thought processes, like worrying about things she had no control over and not prioritising her time with family over work. This helped her overcome the hurdles she was facing. And it gave her the courage to keep going. She told us that if she hadn't leaned into the smarter ways of working, "I don't think I would be here now. I think I would've given up a long time ago." Have you ever felt the same way? That you wanted to give up and walk away?

Jodie is now enjoying the shift from hustle to happy. Her business and team continue to grow, her mum is back in the business with more flexibility than she had before, and the best part? Jodie now takes time for herself. She's doubled her exercise routine, very rarely works on the weekends and enjoys me time (a concept that felt very foreign and unavailable to her at first). She now takes regular holidays and the first holiday she took was the first time in five years that she was uncontactable. It was amazing for her. She recharged her batteries and revelled in not having to worry about anyone but herself.

Jodie almost didn't carve out the time to lean into the smart business growth approach we shared with her because she was time poor, like really time poor! But in the end, she realised she just had to make time. Otherwise, she would have walked out and shut down the business, feeling like she was letting down the twenty-five people who worked for her, as well as her mum who started the business twenty-five years earlier.

PART TWO.

How Do We Get There?

It's time to learn the blueprint for having a thriving business. A pivotal point is understanding what beautiful chaos and destructive chaos is in business and the impact that each has on positive, negative and chronic stress. Knowing this helps navigate the tides of business to make sure you and your team are embracing beautiful chaos and positive stress for growth. This is part of what cultivates a thriving culture and allows you to forge a path towards your true north. Your true north being the ultimate place where all areas of business and life meet to fulfil your business and personal vision.

We want to give you a simple process you can implement right away for your business planning and big picture strategy so that you can lay the foundations, optimise for growth and accelerate results. When there's a clear path, your (and your team's) true north is more easily accessible. It also means you focus on higher quality problems and better-quality conversations pointing towards the big outcomes in business.

Strategy alone will not create sustainable business growth, it's the people that bring this to life. Bringing the peak performance principles of culture, operating rhythms and skills into the mix allows you to develop a sixth sense. Imagine how good it would feel to be confident in your team's ability to perform without needing you to be present. Ultimately you want to move the doers in your team to become decision-makers, allowing you to step back and get on the balcony of your business.

We're going to show you why you don't need another time management tool, what to do instead, how to get more space and grace in your day, and how to know the difference between busy and healthy hustle so that you can start living more.

All this matters because to create a business by design and live life on your own terms, you need the tools to help you succeed. If you don't do anything differently, you'll continue to be stuck in the busy trap *and* in business chaos.

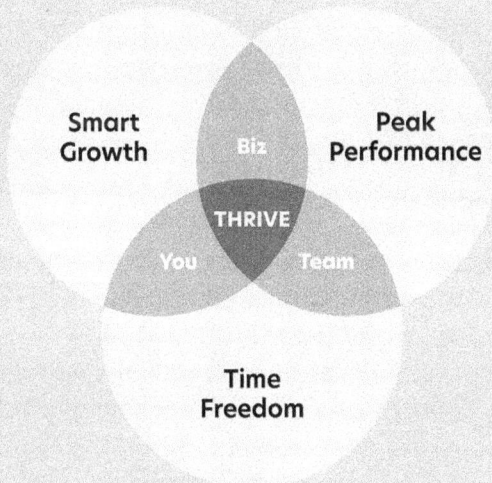

Figure 2 – Thrive Business Model

We've said it before and we'll say it again – we're completely obsessed with helping your business thrive, your team thrive, and *you* thrive too! And the Thrive Business Model (see Figure 2) is the framework that gets you there. It's the blueprint for you to grow smart, not hard. It's what will move your business from chaos to clarity and shine the light on opportunities for growth that could otherwise be easily missed.

The Thrive Business Model highlights three critical parts to healthy hustle. Here's what we'll explore together in the following chapters:

1. **Smart growth.**

    Working smarter, not harder when it comes to growing your business requires you to have a fresh approach to your sales and business planning (Chapter 3).

2. **Peak performance.**

    Peak performance principles and understanding the natural behavioural styles of your people cultivates a culture of high performance allowing your team to step up, so that you can step back (Chapter 4).

3. **Time freedom.**

    Ultimately time freedom means choice. Choice on where and how you want to spend your precious time in this one precious life. With only 4,000 weeks in a lifetime (if you're lucky enough to make it to eighty) why wouldn't you want to embrace the tools that will give you time back to enjoy life right now (Chapter 5).

Now here's the thing ... you can't get to time freedom without **first** passing through smart growth and peak performance. It's the power of the three in that order that makes this a supercharger for you and your business (see figure 3).

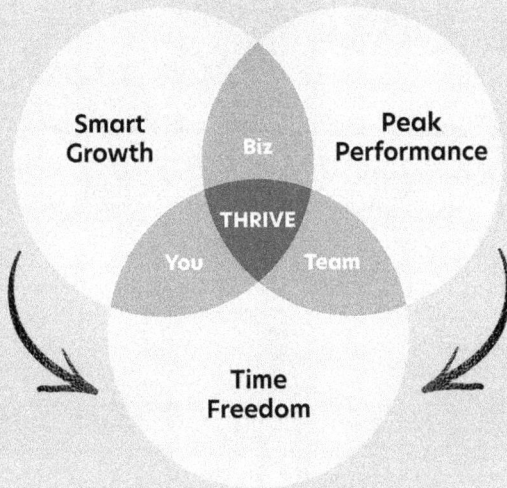

Figure 3

The trap many business owners and leaders fall into is that they try to get to time freedom before establishing smart growth and peak performance strategies. It's only when you have solid smart growth systems in place (such as an established sales ecosystem) and an empowered and autonomous team performing at their best (peak performance) that you have the space to embrace time freedom. One can't be met without the other.

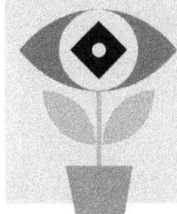

CHAPTER THREE.

Smart Growth: Chaos to Clarity

STEPPING BACK

In 2020, when we were all in the midst of Covid, Christine was facing some big challenges. Home schooling two teenagers while running an established business and navigating the transition of face-to-face to online was enough to flirt with the limitations of healthy and unhealthy stress. On top of this, she had five close family members (including her mum) pass away in a three-month period and was unable to attend most of their funerals in person – as you can imagine, this was a tipping point.

Juggling all the balls and trying to look after her family, her business, and the people around her, there simply wasn't time to grieve or focus on herself. It was one thing on top of the next on top of the next. Remember those days when we'd switch on the news each morning and see the death toll and pandemic statistics grow in real-time in front of our eyes? So many unknowns, so much uncertainty.

Her business was impacted, with a significant loss of income, and her kids were living with a different version of their mum. A less happy, frustrated and sad person. And then she was diagnosed with inflammatory bowel disease. Christine wholly believes this diagnosis was related to the cumulative chronic stress and the toxicity in her body from not eating well, not sleeping well and drinking alcohol more heavily. She was barely surviving.

Our bodies have an innate understanding of what we need at any given time and can heal themselves if we just stop and listen. We need to stop and listen to those whispers and take action that will support us as opposed to letting our body and our mind scream at us, ending up in a situation where we're unwell and unable to look after anyone else.

As a health coach and health advocate, this was confronting for Christine to deal with. She knew she had to do something dramatic to shift the situation. She realised she needed to step away, take a break, and just remove herself from everything. So, she packed her kids and dog up in a caravan and travelled country-and-coast for four months. Devices were switched off, beach walks and ocean swims happened daily, she started to take better care of what she absorbed not only in her body (nourishing food) but also in her mind (not getting pulled into the whirlwind of traditional and social media). She gave herself space. Time to grieve, cry, or whatever was needed in the moment. She gave herself permission to just be and not do.

Christine realised that without taking care of herself, she couldn't take care of the things around her – family, business, team, clients, community. If we're not looking after ourselves, then everything around us is going to be affected. The bold move that Christine has implemented since then, which we encourage you to do with the True North Framework (more info to come further in this chapter), is that she incorporates her version of 'prioritise life' into her quarterly business planning. She has her list of business activities, as well as health and self-care activities that help her to be a more whole and happy human and, therefore, a better businessperson. She sets significant boundaries to protect her health, wealth and family.

The result? She now has a thriving business, thriving family and thriving life.

Could things have been different for Christine if she'd prioritised life and herself just as much as her business earlier? Chances are with the magnitude of things life was throwing at her, she still would've experience chronic stress, BUT would her road to recovery have been easier? Could she have avoided the health diagnosis? There's no saying what would've happened, and we can't live in the past of regret or wonder. What we can do is start creating the changes needed today, just like Christine did!

A great starting point is being able to identify the difference between positive and negative stress to ensure the psychological safety* of you and your team. And to make sure your business planning prioritises both personal and business goals as much as each other.

BEAUTIFUL CHAOS

It's a known fact that business is chaotic at times. And sometimes that's okay. In fact, it can be an important part of the healthy hustle. It's the beautiful chaos that's often the impetus for massive action. It's what gives us energy and inspiration to keep going, try new things and work towards being the best we can be. Beautiful chaos is energy, growth, riding the wild side and seeing where it takes us. But there's a fine line between beautiful and destructive chaos. The difference? Beautiful chaos has a plan, a compass, a guide and a strategic direction that the business is going in. Beautiful chaos will lead you to momentum. Destructive chaos on the other hand happens when there's no clarity of direction and can lead to negative stress and burnout.

Success Formula:

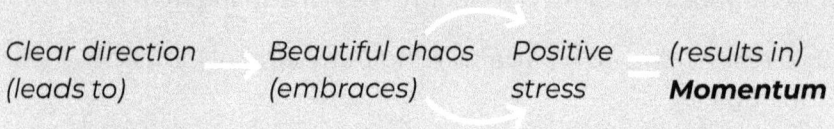

Clear direction (leads to) → Beautiful chaos (embraces) Positive stress = (results in) **Momentum**

Defeat Formula:

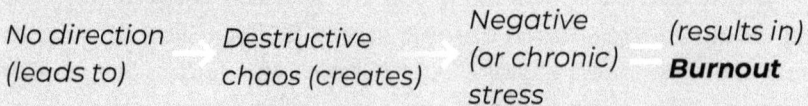

No direction (leads to) → Destructive chaos (creates) → Negative (or chronic) stress (results in) **Burnout**

---

* Team psychological safety is a shared belief held by members of a team that it's okay to take risks, to express their ideas and concerns, to speak up with questions, and to admit mistakes — all without fear of negative consequences.- Amy Edmondson, the Harvard Business School professor and author of *The Fearless Organization*, who coined the phrase "team psychological safety,"

Beautiful chaos takes healthy stress to the limits of productivity and positive change.

Prolonged destructive chaos leads to damaging, unhealthy stress.

To make sure you stay in the zone of the Success Formula (momentum) and away from the Defeat Formula (burnout), you need to:

1. Have clarity and direction in your business via a strategic business plan.
2. Know the difference between healthy (positive) and unhealthy (negative) stress – and the warning signs.

And we're going to help you with both!

First up, not having a simple, solid business plan in place leads to destructive chaos, overwhelm and unnecessary pressure for you and the entire business. Imagine going for a hike in the bush without a GPS or a map. Without preparation and taking a helicopter view of your track, you could exert a lot of energy, not know the direction you're going or how long it will take to get there. You won't know how much you need to conserve your energy, water and food to make it to the destination safely. Not knowing these critical aspects of the journey takes away from you enjoying the experience. When you're distracted by basic survival factors, you miss opportunities, and you miss the chance to enjoy the view as you go along, no matter how hard the hike might get.

As I write this, I think back to when my sisters and I hiked around Hamilton Island. This meant getting up at the crack of dawn, no small feat for this gal who is well known for *not* being in the 5 am Club. But because we had a GPS, a plan, and a compass (known these days as an iPhone) I could see the benefit of getting out of my comfort zone, even before we set off.

What we thought was going to be a 12 km roundtrip ended up being 16 km. It was hard yakka at times, even when it felt like I'd taken my millionth step (no dramatisation here, if you know, you know!), I never considered giving up. Because we had a plan and the tools to help us succeed, we could enjoy the rewards, choose detours, spend more time at some of the incredibly beautiful spots and fully soak in the experience. Leaning into the unknown and the sense of adventure became easier because we ultimately knew that we were on the right track.

This is the same for your business. Your plan is your compass that will either take you directly to your true north or allow for beautiful detours like swimming at hidden beaches, which for your business could be finding untapped markets or sparking creative ideas for new ways to serve your clients. If you're too busy focusing on the dangers or figuring out what direction you're heading, you won't have the mental capacity to focus on higher quality solutions or notice the opportunities, or the landscape around you.

Not having a plan is what leads to destructive chaos. Beautiful chaos is having the reassurance of your compass (your guide) and allows you to look up from where you're stepping to get a bird's eye view of what else is happening around you.

The best part of all this? It doesn't have to be complex or difficult. It can be easy and fun. You can get your whole team onboard and work on it together. Gone are the days of locking yourself in a dingy office for weeks on end building a death by PowerPoint presentation that will become irrelevant a month after it's finished!

EYE OF THE STORM

The second part of staying in momentum, besides clarity and direction, is knowing the difference between positive and negative stress. Each person's stress threshold is unique but there are some common threads you can benchmark yourself and your team against.

Positive Stress

According to Dr Marisa Menchola (a board-certified clinical neuropsychologist), stress is a natural, adaptive, built-in response that prepares us for action, both physically and mentally. Positive, healthy stress should feel like, *Okay, this is going to be hard but I can do this, here we go.*

A positive stress response can have a welcome impact on energy, focus, and drive. Ideally, when the task or project is complete or the problem is solved, the threat (i.e. task or project) passes, and our cortisol levels fall. The parasympathetic nervous system – the 'brake' – dampens the stress response. We can then return to a calm state.

Negative Stress

Managing an excessive workload alongside unrealistic deadlines can exacerbate stress levels, particularly if it's over a long period. It feels like there's no light at the end of the tunnel and is never ending.

The relentless pressure takes its toll and is exacerbated even further if you or your team members are feeling stretched in other areas of life. The majority of Australians feel that stress impacts their physical health (72%) and mental health (64%), but very few reported seeking professional help. This is important for you to keep in mind as a business leader:

How are you creating a safe space for your team to ask for help? What example are you setting with your own stress behaviours?

Signs of Negative Stress

- Making mistakes on simple things you or the team normally do with ease.
- Simple things become hard, little things become impossible.
- Changes in self-care essentials like sleep quality, appetite, energy levels.

If you're not aware of your and your team's stress levels, it can lead to negative stress, and this is where chronic stress can take hold. Chronic stress impacts almost every system in our bodies and can lead to serious health problems. And sadly, chronic stress has become accepted as a normal part of being a busy business owner and leader.

Dr Menchola points out that people often believe chronic (aka long-lasting) stress is normal, "That going through life sleep-deprived, skipping meals, tossing and turning in the middle of the night, and having stress-induced headaches for years is just 'the way things are,' this is just what it's like to be an adult, a parent, a worker, or a caregiver."

This has become the norm! How did we let this happen on our watch?!

You have a chance to change (and save) the lives of your team members and lead by example for all the people that look to you as a leader in business and your community. For the sake of them, you must break the cycle that says this is the norm.

Think we're being dramatic? Christine Boucher, a health coach with twenty years of nursing experience weighed in on this topic when we interviewed her for our podcast. She worked in cardiothoracic intensive care, looking after chronically sick people with heart disease, stroke and diabetes, who were getting bypass surgeries and very invasive procedures. From continuously reading the notes, Christine could see how that trajectory happened. Poor, sedentary lifestyles, inactivity, smoking or drinking heavily, overwhelm, stress and poor nutrition were the things that accumulated to the demise of their health and wellbeing.

These massive, invasive procedures don't only impact the individual, they also impact their families – families that are holding the hands of loved ones in their darkest hours, with so much distress. It impacts their workplace because they take time off work. It impacts the community and, also, the economy. With the average stay in intensive care costing $4,000 per day back in 2019, it's a significant cost to the health care system.

Some interesting (astounding) stats Christine shared with us:

- 94%, or more than 9 in 10 workers, have chronic stress at work.
- The financial impact of employee turnover due to burnout can cost between 30% to 150% of the wage of the employee, with the average wage in Australia being $100,000.
- 75-90% of all doctor's office visits are for stress-related ailments and complaints.

Having a clear direction for you and your team reduces destructive chaos and, therefore, reduces the chance of negative (or chronic) stress in your life. It also gives your business a better chance of survival the longer your business is around – remember the stat we mentioned earlier, 80% of businesses fail within twenty years and one of the main reasons is lack of strategy. Enough said.

At the end of the day, having a solid (and simple) business plan will not only help the health of your business, but also the health of you and your people. It will move you away from the Defeat Formula (pain and burnout) towards the Success Formula (pleasure and momentum). And it will allow you to play in the space of beautiful chaos, which is where the magic happens.

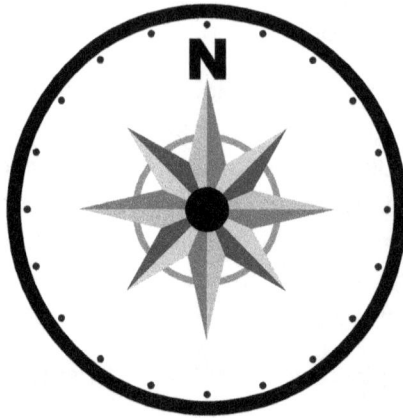

Defining Your True North

THE PAY-OFF

There are three big benefits to using what we call the True North Framework (you'll get the full breakdown in the following pages). **The first is transparency and empowerment.** As the business owner, you have full transparency over what each leader is focusing on, and so everyone has clarity on what's needed to move the boat faster. This means you can get untangled from the weeds and focus on the visionary aspects of your business. You'll finally have the time for blue skies, creative thinking and getting on the balcony to get a helicopter view of your business instead of getting bogged down in unnecessary detail.

You can trust your team to know what to do and, with weekly check-ins, you can support and guide them to stay on track while leaving them to it and giving them space. The best part? You don't have to do the grunt work. Everyone in the team knows who does what, and there's an opportunity for each person to present back to the team how they're tracking, their wins and their learnings. And if this doesn't create an autonomous empowered team, we don't know what does!

The **second big benefit is that you are embedding a holistic approach to thriving in business and life** within the systems of your business. Including 'prioritise life' goals in your planning keeps in focus what's important outside of work. Because you are more than just your work! Doing this with your leaders is a hugely impactful way to engage your leadership team and bring them along for the ride in a way a lot of other businesses don't. Recently we ran a quarterly review with a client and one of their new leaders, his first week in the business, joined in. The feedback he later gave was that he was positively taken aback at how much thought and significance was given to ensuring boundaries and self-care were prioritised as much as business as usual business goals. He'd never experienced this in a workplace before. Right off the bat he could see that culture and people matter at his new place of work. It sets you apart from other employers, and you'll have a happier and more productive workforce.

The **third big benefit** of following this method is that the ripple effect is massive. **You'll be at the forefront of changing the perspective** of chronic stress being the 'norm' for yourself and those around you.

And if that wasn't already enough, there's no doubt in our mind, this process will hold you more accountable to prioritise your own life outside of work. Remember, boss watchers don't just hear what you say, they watch what you do. Baking in prioritising life into your business planning makes sure you're doing just that. You are prioritising your life just as much as your business!

We know that lack of direction leads to an environment of unresourceful destructive chaos, negative (which can lead to chronic) stress, and at the very least an unproductive environment for you and your team to work in. When you define your true north (and give your leaders and team the chance to do the same), you can move away from unhealthy stress. You can clarify what really matters and make sure you're all moving in the same direction. You'll experience chaos in business, but it will be beautiful chaos that you revel in, and it will drive momentum and outcomes. Not only will you lay the foundations of productivity, but you'll also be able to optimise and accelerate with ease being at the forefront, leading the change that's needed in the business world right now. A true example of living healthy hustle.

DEFINING YOUR TRUE NORTH – THE PROCESS

Defining and redefining the next phase of growth and success for you and the business gives you clarity on your true north. Your true north becomes the anchor point and source of truth for you and your team's decisions, actions and categories of success. By implementing the True North Framework, Michael and his Co-Directors went from each running their own strategy and trying to do different things in the business, to being aligned with the vision and goals of the business and understanding the impact of the business on their own personal life goals. This meant they could support each other in embedding the systems to set them up for success. They were able to work their way through, implementing a system that allowed them to identify their six-monthly Wildly Important Goals (WIGs) and get on with it in ninety-day sprints and fortnightly touch points for accountability. The results spoke for themselves.

Let us take you through the True North Framework step-by-step.

Link to access all resources here ⬇

www.nickymiklos.com/book-resources

INTRODUCING THE TRUE NORTH FRAMEWORK

This framework gives you clarity on where you want to go and why it matters, and makes sure you have a holistic approach to balancing business and life priorities.

The True North Framework includes:

- Plan on a Page (PoP).
- 90-day Sprints.
- Monthly Milestones.
- Weekly Top 5s.

Step 1: Lay the Five Foundations with your PoP

A PoP is simply a plan on a page. We've been using this process in our own business and with our clients for years, so it's tried and tested with proven success. There are five key elements to your PoP. Remember to download a template at:

www.nickymiklos.com/book-resources

1. **Vision**. Break this down to a Business Vision (define the big-picture vision of your business, in two or three sentences) and a Personal Vision (define your personal vision, why you do what you do, who you do it for and what matters to you most).

2. **Revenue target**. Make sure you have a full-year revenue (sales) target.

3. **Profit target**. What annual profit percentage are you striving for?

4. **6-month WIGs**. Outline in short sentences two to four Wildly Important Goals (WIGs) that you want to achieve, outside of the business as usual running of the business.

   As Chris McChesney, Sean Covey and Jim Huling, authors of *The 4 Disciplines of Execution*, agree, "The more you try to do, the less you actually accomplish." This highlights the importance of choosing only two to four WIGs instead of trying to improve everything at once.

5. **90-day outcomes.** Clarify the two to four big outcomes that need to be achieved over the next ninety days to stay on track for achieving the WIGs.

You'll find downloadable templates for business owners and leaders at

www.nickymiklos.com/book-resources

Step 2: Optimise for Growth – 90-day Outcomes

We have been fortunate to work with many businesses over the years and we've identified the patterns that make or break success. Successful business owners and leaders know that to optimise their results, it's best to break down the WIGs into four critical areas:

1. **Business growth**. What's one goal you want to achieve specifically to **grow your business** over the next six to twelve months (above the day-to-day business as usual).

   Examples could be onboarding new clients, client segmentation targets, breaking into a new industry, a merger or acquisition, additional marketing campaigns, revising current sales processes.

2. **Manage money**. What's one goal you want to achieve specifically around **managing money** in the business over the next six to twelve months (above the day-to-day business as usual).

   Examples could be implementing a profit planning strategy, increasing average cost per sale, reviewing pricing and packaging, reducing costs within the business through intentional

spending, reducing the number of days it takes to receive payment from your debtors, creating a cash flow planner.

3. **Peak performance**. What's one goal you want to achieve specifically to **increase performance in the team** over the next six to twelve months (above the day-to-day business as usual).

   Examples could be targeted training and development workshops throughout the quarter covering specific topics, introducing individual development plans, embedding a consistent cadence of coaching for the team, revisiting the operating rhythms and regular team communication touchpoints.

4. **Prioritise life**. What's one goal you want to achieve specifically around **prioritising life** just as much as business over the next six to twelve months (above the day-to-day business as usual).

   Examples could be not working in the evenings to be more present with the family, personal KPIs like date night with wifey/hubby/partner/ bestie/doggo, health and wellbeing goals, fun activities or hobbies you've been thinking about (true story: a couple of years ago my goal was to increase my axe throwing score and, I gotta

tell ya, it worked!). Get creative with this one and have fun with it. Think about the things you wish you had time for, this will give you clues on what your prioritised life goals could (not should) be.

✔ TOP TIP

If the word 'should' comes up as you're setting your prioritised life WIGs and big outcomes, it could be an indicator that it's not something you *really* want to do but rather something you feel obligated to do. You could be setting yourself up for failure straight out of the gate before you have even started. Challenge your thinking and connect with what will bring you joy.

An example could be, if it's exercise and you feel you 'should' be doing more, how can you reframe it so exercise becomes something you *want* to do? Maybe it's the type of exercise that needs to change.

Step 3: Accelerate Results

To keep your finger on the pulse, regularly track and measure your PoP. It's much easier to do this when you break down your 90-day outcomes into manageable monthly milestones and a weekly five-to-thrive.

This keeps your 6-month WIGs and 90-day big outcomes in focus, giving you and your team the best possible chance of achieving success.

Monthly Milestones

Each quarter when you're completing your PoP, also complete your monthly milestones so that you're starting to get clear on the actionable tasks needed each month to move you towards your goals. Make sure that within your monthly milestones you're focusing equally on business growth goals, managing money, peak performance and prioritising life.

This is how you maintain a consistent focus on smart business growth covering intentional sales and profit; building an empowered and autonomous team; and establishing time freedom standards for all people in the business.

MONTH 1 (30 DAYS):			
Business Growth 1.	**Manage Money/** 1.	**Prioritise Life** 1.	**Peak Performance** 1.
2.	2.	2.	2.
3.	3.	3.	3.
MONTH 2 (60 DAYS):			
Business Growth 1.	**Manage Money/** 1.	**Prioritise Life** 1.	**Peak Performance** 1.
2.	2.	2.	2.
3.	3.	3.	3.
MONTH 3 (90 DAYS):			
Business Growth 1.	**Manage Money/** 1.	**Prioritise Life** 1.	**Peak Performance** 1.
2.	2.	2.	2.
3.	3.	3.	3.

THIS CYCLE BEGINS: _____ ENDS: _____

Monthly **MILESTONES**

www.businesstogether.com.au   www.nickymiklos.com

Download this template at
www.nickymiklos.com/book-resources

Weekly Five-to-Thrive

In a worldwide study by the Harvard Business Review in 2019, professionals with the highest productivity scores tended to plan their work based on their top priorities, and then acted with a definite objective.

Every week, check in with how you're progressing with your monthly milestones and your 90-day outcomes so you can prioritise your top five tasks for the week. These should be above and beyond the day-to-day business as usual and help move the dial towards your wildly important goals. Like the monthly milestones, make

sure that within your top fives, one is geared towards achieving your business growth, managing money, peak performance and prioritising life goals.

Stephen Covey famously said in his book First Things First, "You have to decide what your highest priorities are and have the courage – pleasantly, smilingly, non-apologetically – to say 'no' to other things. And the way you do that is by having a bigger 'yes' burning inside."

Weekly **FIVE-TO-THRIVE**™

DATE:

TOP 5	#1 Business Growth	#2	#3	#4 Manage Money	#5 Prioritise Life
PLAN IT	MON	TUES	WED	THURS	FRID
	Connect with...	Connect with...	Connect with...	Connect with...	Connect with...

FINISH IT Reflect on last week	Wins	Learns	How You're Tracking to 90 Day Outcomes:
	1.	1.	
	2.	2.	What I'll improve on next week:
	3.	3.	

Download this template at
www.nickymiklos.com/book-resources

In this case, your burning yeses are your top five that (thanks to the True North Framework) are clearly linked to the vision of the business. They're the things that no matter what, must get done in the week, which helps you prioritise, set boundaries and shift your mindset and beliefs around where you 'should' be spending your time.

Be sure to get your leadership team to follow this same process and share weekly, monthly and quarterly updates with each other in your team meetings. You'll get to celebrate the smaller wins along the way and brainstorm ideas together to overcome challenges and blockers, as well as see each other's progress.

Going the Distance

Michael (who we mentioned earlier) and his fellow directors were years into their business when it occurred to them that they weren't putting enough focus on the 'end goal'. They knew they needed to make the business work for them, and not the other way around, because without them, the business wouldn't succeed.

Michael found that there were times when he was left wondering how to stay focused and motivated. The business often felt like it was on a mouse wheel instead of moving forward because the ways of working were reactionary and constant, never having a moment to stop and reflect. Have you ever caught yourself so deep in the whirlwind that you felt you were stuck?

Michael and his colleagues realised that in order for them to go the distance, they also needed to have a focus on the things they enjoyed in life. The things that gave them energy. So, with a bit of guidance and support, they got to work on defining their individual true norths. They got clear on why success in the business mattered to each of them. What it was all for. And this became the link between the day-to-day running of their business and the future they were each creating!

Having a blend of both business and personal goals (aka WIGs) helps to keep a spotlight on – and to prioritise – your life goals. Because these are the goals that can be so easily put to the side when running a business. Following this process helped Michael and his fellow business owners realise the value of stepping back to look at a bigger perspective. Through this perspective they could start to see the progress they were making and start to live their own true norths ... winning in both business and life!

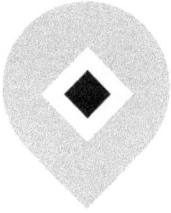

BONUS.

LET'S TALK SALES – THE BACKBONE OF BUSINESS

Okay, okay, it's no secret we love talking all things sales, and so it would be remiss not to talk about sales when talking about healthy hustle. Sales is a critical component of smart business growth and it often gets a bad rap. It's seen as the pushy car-salesman-style necessary evil of business. And yet, sales is the backbone of your business.

> **Regardless of service or product type, industry, or company size, the growth of a business lives and dies by the success of its sales.**

When sales are strong, you can focus on profit planning, growth and investing in your team. But without sales, your business is at best a hobby or at worst a financial burden.

Underdogs Rising

There's no greater example of underdogs rising when Gemma's sales team did their 'Fight for Digital' at the run home to end of financial year. Imagine this, two weeks out from end of year, pipeline was drying up, the team had left no stone unturned and there was only $70K to hit their $12M target. To call defeat now wasn't an option for this team of go-getters and sales superstars. We facilitated a hot seat mentoring session with sales, product and operations leaders, and a plan was formed taking into account increased sales activities, increased tracking, getting the team on board and excited to measure and monitor the progress daily and celebrating all the wins – large and small. They took the plan to the wider team for additional ideas, brainstorming and to get all hands on deck. The team executed with urgency and evaluated results over the two-week period. And what d'you know, they pulled it off, banking another $150K, delivering $80K *over* their full year target.

The secret to their success? Well, there were many moving parts.

- It was no coincidence that this team's annual engagement results were not only above the average across the company, but also among the highest in the company.
- They didn't give up. Even when the odds were stacked against them, they fought till the end.
- They had a collective purpose that every single person was motivated to go for.
- They did it for each other. It wasn't about the singular; it was about the collective. Those who had already hit their individual target were still highly motivated to dig in for their colleagues.
- The groundwork was done. Of course, it wasn't just about what they'd achieved in those two weeks. They could pull it off because they had installed peak performance sales principles throughout the entire year to build on.

In the words of Henry Ford, "If everyone is moving forward together, then success takes care of itself."

Leaving Money on the Table

Sales can feel chaotic in business. Often there's no system or structure, and team members could be more proactive in getting out there and talking to clients, finding other ways to help them. Instead, they're reactive, waiting for the phone to ring (or email to come in) and leaving money on the table. And let's face it, among all the chaos it's hard to find the time to nurture connections, relationships, warm leads and prospects. I mean, it's damn busy right!?

Healthy hustle is having a good sales ecosystem in place that allows you as the leader to step back without halting the growth of the business. It means you can feel confident the business is moving away from a *passive* sales approach and towards an *active* sales approach. Let's break it down together.

A good sales ecosystem has three elements: sales systems, sales strategy and sales skills.

Sales Systems

In a lot of businesses, the systems are ambiguous. The 'what' that the team are striving for and the 'how' they'll get there are vague and inconsistent. If this is you, no wonder you still need to be so hands on.

Instead, you want to focus on laying out the roadmap for the team to know exactly what they're shooting for and put the right systems in place to support the team. As our client James B says, "After years in business, I realised I'm not as important as I thought I was." He came to understand that "If you're that

95

important, maybe your business is not structured correctly." And sales systems are a key player in this.

Sales Strategy

Another sales gap a lot of businesses are navigating is unintentionally neglecting their clients and potential clients (leads). It's not intentional neglect but neglect all the same. Success is replicable and with the right strategy in place, success is inevitable. We know that the busy trap is in play and our salespeople are doing more with less, juggling just as many balls as we are! So, make it easy for them, set them up for success with a strategic approach that looks at existing clients, referral opportunities and lead generation to make sure your team is consistently nurturing clients and relationships instead of neglecting them.

Sales Skills

The business owners and sales leaders we work with and talk to often feel like their teams are at times reactive and order taking, leaving money on the table. They're waiting for the opportunities to come to them, instead of being proactive in finding them. I've led and coached sales teams through some of the most challenging market conditions, including the 2009 global financial crisis, during and following the global pandemic, and in high stakes, fast-paced changing environments like the movement from traditional to digital media, and the transition from bricks and mortar to online businesses. I have a saying I take with me always:

If it ain't coming in, we're going out to get it!

This is the true sign of an autonomous and high-performing sales team. They're not waiting for leads and opportunities to come to them, they're being proactive and seeking them out. The best sales leaders and salespeople shine when times are tough, it's easy when the market is easy.

When the Hustle is Healthy

Of course there's a financial benefit to installing a solid sales ecosystem, there can't not be. But the other benefit that you may not have thought about is the effect on the health and wellbeing of your sales leaders and team. A study found that **67% of workers in business development and sales were close to experiencing burnout** because of long working hours, a dense workload, and feeling required to always be 'on'. In the HubSpot 2024 sales trends report, 54% of sales pros say selling has been harder this year than it was before. Year-on-year there have been more and more challenges to traverse in the world of sales.

Having a sales ecosystem means sales are evergreen and ever-growing, requiring less effort (hello healthy hustle), and that's going to give you an upturn and increase in conversions and sales revenue. Guaranteed! Follow the bouncing ball and results will follow. Even a solid nurture strategy on its own has an immediate and direct impact on your bottom line effectively *and* efficiently.

Acquiring new customers costs approximately five to seven times more than retaining an existing one. What's the average cost for you to acquire a new client?

If you don't already know, take some time to figure this out – consider marketing costs per lead, time to convert each lead, lead conversion and drop off rates, including how many touchpoints by who (and the relevant hourly rate). Include any costs of goods sold, onboarding touchpoints and gifts. There's a lot of time and money involved in acquiring new clients. Now think about the cost involved in nurturing your existing clients and compare the two. There's so much opportunity to support and serve the people you already have in your world, your raving fans. Healthy hustle involves looking at low hanging fruit – remember this is about doubling your results, with only half the effort!

Another shortcut to improving bottom line revenue results is knowing current sales market challenges and trends. This allows you to prepare and plan for them, making sure the hustle stays healthy. Here's the top five sales trends we're seeing that'll be sticking around for a while:

- **Sales cycles are longer** with more decision-makers needing to be involved in the sales conversations (tighter budgets will do that!).

- **Conversion rates are lower**. One contributor to this is because salespeople are giving up before getting a definitive yes, no or maybe. Eighty percent of effective sales requires at least five follow up calls after the first meeting, yet 44% of people give up after the first try. How many follow-ups are in your sales process?

- **Distrust is more widespread** than ever before. With the growing amount of scams, spamming and Artificial Intelligence (AI), it's completely understandable that people don't know who, where or what to trust! We certainly don't like answering our phone to unknown numbers – do you? Yet another reason it's getting tougher out there.

- **People are struggling** (your clients and your team alike). People are grappling with all that is going on in the world, on top of the ever-pressing need to keep up with the pace of work that's become the norm. And so again, it's no wonder salespeople are even more hesitant than usual about doing sales reach outs for fear of being 'annoying' or 'intrusive' (their words, not ours).

- **Sales has a bad rap**. In a sales workshop we ran recently, 75% of people polled felt that sales is a necessary evil or something they avoid as much as possible. How your team feels about selling your products and services has a huge impact on the bottom line. You can have the best tools, strategies and systems in place but it's their perception of sales that will subconsciously help or hinder their results.

If this era is teaching us anything, it's how to be more resilient, consistent and creative when it comes to establishing and nurturing leads, prospects and client relationships.

Passive to Active

How confident and creative would you say your team is when it comes to contact types and reach outs. A great way to prioritise action is by looking at hot, warm and cold leads. A lot of people want to avoid making cold contacts and reach outs because it feels the most awkward. Fair enough! The best way to deal with this is to get great at nurturing warm and hot leads so there's no need for cold contacts. We'd say that's a smart way to grow sales. But in reality, most leads are either cold or warm. Hot can be a rare find, which is why nurturing is such an important part of the active sales process!

✔ TOP TIP:

In case cold, warm and hot leads are new concepts for you, we've summarised them here.

- **Cold leads** are those that don't know you or your business. They're possibly at the awareness phase of the buyer's journey and are not yet ready to buy.

- **Warm leads** know you or your business or you have a mutual connection. This is where referral magic happens. Referrals are a great low hanging fruit opportunity: 91% of customers say they'd give referrals and yet only 11% of salespeople ask for them. Money left on the table, people! Warm leads are at the consideration phase of the buyer's journey, they're looking at and considering their options.

- **Hot leads** have nothing to do with how good looking they are and everything to do with the fact that they're ready to buy. They know who you are and how you can help. They're at the decision phase of the buyer's journey, deciding who's the best fit for their needs.

Okay, so if the goal is to nurture cold-to-warm, warm-to-hot leads and relationships, here's four proven sales strategies for you and your team to explore:

1. Sales and marketing work together, not against each other

Sales and marketing need to be in sync to get the best results and can lead to 38% higher sales win rates, drive more than 200% revenue growth and 36% higher customer retention. We've seen too many times the negative impact on businesses when sales and marketing don't talk to each other. There's an incredibly symbiotic relationship between the two. Make sure that your ideal message is going to your ideal client when attracting (marketing) and qualifying (sales) leads. That the conversation to convert is seamless (sales) and meets the promise that brought them to you in the first place (marketing).

2. Move away from the 'traditional' sales process to an 'active' sales process

The typical sales process involves waiting for an email or a phone call, having a meeting with a cold start (i.e., not knowing much, if anything about the prospect), and then emailing a proposal only never to be heard of again. This is where proposal chasing kicks in, and the salesperson could very easily be ghosted. An active sales process has more touch points. It might seem like more work up front, but the pay-off is worth it. Credibility improves, relationships are stronger and there's a higher chance of conversion with minimal-to-no proposal chasing.

Things like qualifying the prospect before setting any meetings, connecting on LinkedIn, sending voice notes or Loom videos and making sure no meeting ends without setting the next meeting will be what transforms the traditional sales process to an active sales process. Even just these few simple additions will give you a greater chance of converting the sale and save your salespeople a heck of a lot of time in the end.

3. Don't just rely on emails to contact and engage people

Have at least five touch points when **establishing** (cold-warm) or **nurturing** (warm-hot) relationships. Too many people rely solely on the odd email. Think about how many emails you get in a day! There's too many. We're not saying don't email ever, just make sure it's a *part of* an overall strategy, *not the only* strategy. Get creative and think outside the box. What will get people's attention? What are your competitors doing to establish and nurture, how can you be different and stand out?

We've listed some strategies our clients use below. What other ideas do you have?

- Connect and engage on your preferred social platform.
- Send voice notes.
- Do personalised videos with tools like Loom video.
- Text messages if appropriate.
- Use email strategically and think about how it will stand out among *aaaall* the other emails in our inboxes.
- Lumpy mail, popping something in the post that will get people curious enough to open it. We've had clients do anything from thank you cards with little packets of Skittles inside, to branded KeepCups, or beautifully printed hardcover books showcasing their portfolio of work.

4. Understand your team's natural selling style

There are a variety of natural sales styles and knowing where your team sits allows you to structure your people's day around their strengths and identify what support they need to develop their sales skills. For example, do they get nervous about doing cold reach outs and contacts? You can help them with a script guide. If motivation is a factor, perhaps schedule an hour of power with the team. Or maybe they get stuck in unnecessary details that stop them from picking up the phone? Coach them on the need-to-knows for the client.

State of Change

I recently came across an article I wrote in 2021, just coming off the back of the global pandemic grenade that had been thrown into people's lives and businesses. What struck me was that it's now years later and I could've written it yesterday. While the circumstances and context are different today, the state of change, uncertainty and fatigue remains.

> There's no doubt about it ... global sadness, fear, uncertainty is in the air these days. Across the world sh*t's going down – in a multitude of ways. And I'm sure you feel it too!
>
> As I watch the news, it blows my mind the ferocity and magnitude of things that are happening yet, while the world seems to be imploding, our mundane routines continue. We still need to cook dinner, buy toilet paper, do the washing, deal with IT issues, do our admin. Gagh! Somehow, we're still expected to carry on as though everything's 'normal' and our business needs to keep running.

This is a great reminder that **change is a constant**.

External market impacts are always going to be an available excuse for people to hide behind instead of getting their sh*t sorted when it comes to being proactive and transparent with their sales systems, strategy and the skills of the team.

Companies that invest in sales training achieve 50% higher net sales per employee and a 12% higher profit margin.

Sales *is* the backbone of any successful business. Having the bones in place to drive active sales will get you further, quicker (and remember, if you want healthy hustle, you want *smart* ways to get further, quicker). You can flesh out your sales systems and strategy with your own brand personality, by leveraging the character and strengths of the individuals within the business. And it allows you to hand over more sales responsibilities to your team, so that you can step back from making money in the business being so reliant on you. What we're talking about here is moving beyond a passive sales approach in the business to having an active one. This is exactly why Gemma's sales team were so successful when they did their 'Fight for Digital' at the run home to EOFY, therefore finishing the year strong and well above target *with* such an actively engaged team.

Now is the time to lean in. The biggest unique selling point of your business is your salespeople, they're at the coalface representing your brand and often the first interaction that prospects and clients have with you. Consider how bucking the current sales trends and implementing best practice systems and strategies can help your business continue to thrive in these wild times.

They Did It Again

Nick, co-owner and co-founder, spent most of the business's fifteen-year history as its key salesperson. However, as he looked to diversify his role and delve into other aspects of the business, he recognised the pressing need to build a robust sales team. With this realisation, he invested significant time and effort in connecting with the right people, reading books and attending seminars. Nick learnt that the team needed a shared understanding and common goals which led him and his wife, Jeni, to seek out a coach who could guide them in building this cohesive team.

For the next three years, Nick and Jeni observed a remarkable transformation in their team. The quarterly total immersion events delivered by Nicky became a cornerstone of their strategy. "The first one we ever did was amazing," Nick recalled. "The team, which had never really worked together in such a collaborative way, felt an incredible surge of energy. The combination of these events and the weekly coaching sessions helped hold the team accountable for their commitments. Our quarterly catchups have become a driving force behind our results."

One of Nick's proudest moments came when he and Jeni took a month-long holiday overseas. During their absence, the sales team, bolstered by Nicky's guidance and accountability, exceeded their Q4 sales targets. This success prompted them to raise the target by another $100K for the next quarter, and once again, the team delivered.

Reflecting on his journey, Nick marvelled at how far they had come from the days when sales relied solely on his efforts. In his words, "It all comes down to teamwork, where everyone understands their role, what they're doing, and what they're contributing."

The team were proactive in leaning into the active sales approach, they got creative and leveraged their natural strengths. They became the champion sales team in their industry *and* had a lot of fun along the way.

CHAPTER FOUR.

Peak Performance: Stepping Off Juggle Street

DECODING HUMAN BEHAVIOUR

Mitz is a successful, well-respected leader who is naturally great at in-depth 1:1 conversations with her people, but small talk was never her natural strength. To her, small talk felt fake and superficial and so it just didn't cross her mind on a Monday morning to walk the floor and chat briefly about the weekend with her team. Doing this wasn't meaningful to her but she was aware enough as a leader to know that it was meaningful for some of her people. It would make them feel acknowledged and seen, and it helped to build rapport.

So, to make sure she could be consistent and remember to do this, she leveraged her natural strength around structure and put it on her checklist. This made sure the task wasn't overlooked and, sure enough, the strategy worked. Eventually it became habit enough that she didn't need to put it on her checklist. Knowing which energy styles are **natural** and which need to be **learnt** for yourself and your leaders is a huge milestone to move towards peak performance.

A big element of not hustling harder is working to your natural strengths to get the best outcome. Return on effort comes into play when we're working with our natural drivers instead of against them. And this goes for all the people in your business.

There's a common misconception that we, as individuals, are unique. That's not true. There are patterns in human behaviour that have been identified, observed and unpacked over the last hundred years. Psychologists and a whole bunch of people much smarter than us have been decoding these patterns and giving us the blueprint of human behaviour. The cheat sheet, if you will, to be able to see and leverage natural strengths and blind spots in people. Understanding why there are things we can do with ease versus other things taking more effort. Tasks we're naturally good at or that take more focus, attention and time.

It's not about right or wrong, good or bad, or about putting people in boxes. It's about acknowledging that there are patterns in how we communicate, how we see (and react to) the world and how we behave. When you choose to learn and see these patterns, you get direct access to the best ways of working for your team.

In 1921, Carl Jung (a Swiss psychiatrist and psychotherapist who founded analytical psychology) observed certain behaviours and patterns of thinking-feeling that fall into four dimensions (most people are typically a mix of two). William Marston* then further developed the work of Jung and illustrated the four-dimension behavioural map. As a result, the four-quadrant thinking of DISC was developed as we know it today.

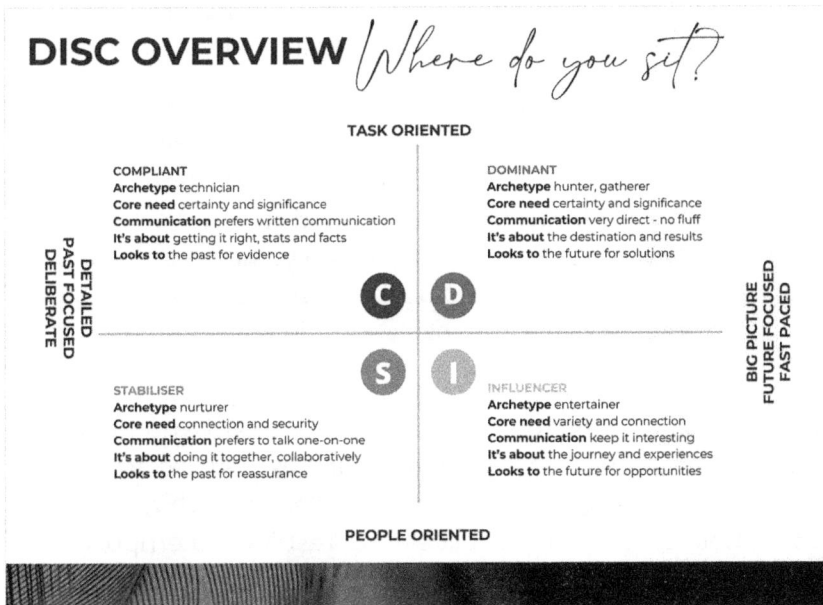

DISC OVERVIEW *Where do you sit?*

TASK ORIENTED

COMPLIANT
Archetype technician
Core need certainty and significance
Communication prefers written communication
It's about getting it right, stats and facts
Looks to the past for evidence

DOMINANT
Archetype hunter, gatherer
Core need certainty and significance
Communication very direct - no fluff
It's about the destination and results
Looks to the future for solutions

C **D**

DETAILED PAST FOCUSED DELIBERATE

BIG PICTURE FUTURE FOCUSED FAST PACED

S **I**

STABILISER
Archetype nurturer
Core need connection and security
Communication prefers to talk one-on-one
It's about doing it together, collaboratively
Looks to the past for reassurance

INFLUENCER
Archetype entertainer
Core need variety and connection
Communication keep it interesting
It's about the journey and experiences
Looks to the future for opportunities

PEOPLE ORIENTED

⬇ **Download this template at**
www.nickymiklos.com/book-resources

---

* Interesting side note: Marston was an American psychologist who, with his wife Elizabeth Holloway, invented an early prototype of the polygraph. He was also a writer and created the character of Wonder Woman with his wife and polyamorous life partner. What a bio!

DISC is not about personality (not who you are) but more about your behavioural preferences. So, are you naturally a big picture thinker or more detail-oriented? Do you like to be front row centre at the party, or behind the scenes taking care of people? Are you inherently more task or people-focused? Are you a visual (see), kinaesthetic (feel) or auditory (hear) learner?

Each person's behavioural style influences the language they use, how they present themselves, and what motivates and inspires them.

It can give clues about what types of tasks they might try to avoid, how they navigate change, and their natural strengths and blind spots related to their individual role in the business

The gift in understanding these behavioural styles is that it separates the human from the behaviour. It's easier to be more forgiving instead of frustrated. You can understand people's perspectives and views of the world, build stronger connections, and have a team that feels valued, driven to succeed and are not only capable of stepping up but they also want to step up and they feel more certain in themselves to do so.

You can leverage natural ways of working and help work on the blind spots to make sure your team members are strengthening their learnt behaviours as well as leveraging their natural strengths. It's the combo deal of both **natural** and **learnt** behaviours that will accelerate results and empower the team member.

> **Natural behaviour:** being that which the individual can do with ease and not as much effort.
>
> **Learnt behaviour:** being that which takes more effort and focus. It can still be done, it just might need more practice, training and support to get there.

An example of natural behaviour is someone who is naturally visionary in their thinking, sees the big picture, and can come up with great ideas and solutions to problems. They're very action oriented and fast-paced, future focused, with a sense of urgency. If they're required to do detailed work that involves analytical thinking, lots of research and data analysis, that's learned behaviour and it will take them more time, focus and attention than someone who has those natural traits. And it might not be as enjoyable for them. It doesn't mean they can't do a great job of it, but their journey to best practice will be different to someone who is naturally that way inclined.

We like to compare it with doing the downward dog for all those yoga-goers out there (stick with us if you're not). Now aside from the people who are naturally very flexible and talented in yoga, for the rest of us mere mortals the downward dog is quite an uncomfortable pose. You've got hands on the floor at the top of your yoga mat, feet flat on the ground towards the other end of the mat and your butt is high in the air. For most people, the first time (and many times after) doing this pose is quite uncomfortable. It's not uncommon for the arms to start shaking, the neck to tense up, the hamstrings to feel tight. Now, this yoga pose is meant to be a rest pose. A rest pose! Hah. There's a lot of focus and attention that needs to happen to stay in that position and they call it a rest pose (we won't repeat the expletives here from when we first heard this). But here's the thing. What we've found is that over time it *does* become easier. It will never be as comfortable and easy as Savasana (known as corpse pose because it literally requires nothing other than lying on your back, with your arms and legs splayed like a corpse – gotta be honest, this one's a fave!). But with practice, endurance and time downward dog does become a different type of comfortable. A comfortable that still requires muscles and conscious awareness to be switched on. The muscles can relax a little, the neck doesn't tense up as much and the stretch in the hammies feels quite good.

So, when we think about natural and learnt behaviours, we think about the corpse pose being like your natural styles (it's easy as and you could stay there all day), and the downward dog being like your learnt behaviours (it'll take more effort and conscious awareness, you might suck at it a bit first but over time you'll get better at it). It becomes an odd type of comfortable.

PEAK PERFORMANCE PRINCIPLES

You thought having a team around you would make your life easier ... but has it?

It wouldn't surprise us if you're putting out more fires than ever before and still feel like you're being pulled in a million different directions. We have a name for this, it's called being on Juggle Street. It's when you're trying to be all things to all people, despite having a team. Juggle Street is the opposite of what we're trying to achieve and working towards with healthy hustle.

Wouldn't it be brilliant if all your team were consistently delivering and exceeding expectations, even when you weren't in the room? They're able to make autonomous decisions before escalating to you and can manage the day-to-day confidently. Well, that my friend is what we call peak performance.

It's only when you (and your team) get off Juggle Street that you can start the move towards peak performance.

Promoting people and getting the org chart right is only the beginning when it comes to building an independent, capable team. You also need to dedicate time and energy to fostering a great culture, having good operating rhythms in place, and developing the skills of your people.

When looking at the critical areas of peak performance, we can break it down to culture, operating rhythms and skills. Overlaying the behavioural styles of DISC will take peak performance to a whole new level. **It's what aligns the rhythm of your people with the rhythm of your business!**

You can have confidence and certainty that your team are delivering to your standard and expectations without having to be present; that if mistakes are made (which they will be), your team are capable and confident enough to fix them and get things back on track, giving your team the chance to exceed your expectations *and* love what they do at the same time.

The principles of peak performance are:

Culture:

Your work environment fosters enjoyment and productivity, allowing the space for your team to thrive in their zone of genius. You prioritise a harmonious blend of work–life balance, encouraging authenticity and individual expression within a safe, supportive space. Your shared vision involves all team members, giving them meaning and purpose to their work. You and your team are living and breathing your shared values and, overall, it's a great place to be.

Operating Rhythms:

You have structured systems for consistent ways of working, onboarding and team communication. This includes regular team meetings, monthly wrap-ups to celebrate achievements and learn from challenges, process guides and manuals on hand, and clarity of roles and expectations. These best practice principles cultivate a cohesive environment and have a positive impact on building a thriving culture.

Skills:

People are the heart of your business. You have a cadence of coaching, training, upskilling and individual development plans in place for your people. This isn't a once-off tick and flick, it's a consistent focus to make sure your people are supported in their ability to deliver on the expectations you've placed on them.

CULTIVATING A THRIVING CULTURE

Sometimes all it takes is a 1% shift or a slight tweak to cultivate a thriving culture that further builds high-performance practices and results. A dedicated focus on culture, operating rhythms and skills all while leaning into the natural strengths within your team will allow you to finally step back from being pulled into the day-to-day whirlwind. It will allow you to finally break the cycles of unhealthy hustle that are holding you (and most likely your team) back.

You'll have the space to get back into your zone of genius, have more family time, or to focus on your next project, whatever the 'next' looks like for you.

Research by McCrindle shows that people are motivated at work by:

- seeing the **positive impact** of their work.
- the **responsibility** they carry.
- **their performance.**

This proves that the more you empower your team and involve them in the process so they're accountable for their performance and can see the impact of their work, the more inspired, engaged and motivated they'll be. And the more pride they'll take in their work. Giving them responsibility and accountability is so damn important.

On the flipside, if things continue to feel out of control, as the 'big boss' you might try to white-knuckle it and hold onto things even tighter. You could find yourself unwillingly micromanaging, which will result in the opposite effect of what you're going for. Micromanaging creates an unhealthy and at times a toxic environment. At its worst, micromanaging can be a form of bullying. It devalues team members and shuts down creativity, blocking new and better ways of doing things. It can negatively affect mental health and burnout rates and there's no doubt it keeps the business leader tethered unnecessarily to details in the business.

Research by Trinity Solutions showed that **85% of people surveyed said morale was negatively impacted due to micro-management, 69% considered a job change** and **36% changed jobs.**

In a nutshell, continuing to *not let go* will disempower and disengage your team and, eventually, your people will leave.

The main reasons leaders hold on to control and don't let go are:

- Perfectionism (no one can do it as well as me).
- Fear (of loss of control).
- Ego and loss of identity (who am I if I'm not needed in the business).

The problem with these reasons for micromanaging is they give a false sense of security and, therefore, keep the business leader stuck. Perfectionism, fear and ego all breed a culture that lacks trust.

Some years ago, we were working with Ben, a corporate leader stepping into a new leadership role. Ben had tried his hand at leadership a few years earlier but it didn't go well. This was his second chance and he really wanted to nail it. But he was having issues with his team. They didn't respect him as a leader, they didn't listen to him, they were late to meetings and distracted in coaching sessions. There was a lot of behind his back chatter and he felt so isolated in his team. He shared that the dynamic was very 'them versus me' and it was hard. It was hard for him and it was hard for his team as they also didn't feel supported.

When we asked Ben if he trusted his team, he looked at us blankly and at first didn't know how to answer the question. That was all the answer we needed. It was clear that the lack of trust and respect was a two-way street. Ben had gone in all guns blazing expecting respect because his title now had 'manager' in it. The lack of trust led to micromanaging, which led to a revolt within the team, and everyone's effort and focus was on the drama instead of what they were there to achieve.

Ben's a not a bad person, his intention wasn't to alienate his team. There was a lot on the line for him in proving he could do this and so his focus was on himself (on being a great leader) instead of them (on how to best support the people in his team). In the end, Ben decided that leadership wasn't for him, but we can't help wondering what could've been different if Ben had focused more on the peak performance principles and understood the individual behavioural drivers of his team members when he first stepped into that role. If he could've cultivated a thriving culture, implemented the principles we're talking about now around the culture he was creating, operating rhythms, skills and uncovering natural strengths of people ... would it have had a different outcome? For him it was too late, but for you and your leaders it isn't. We invite you to consider the impact that the peak performance principles combined with the four behavioural styles can have on your business.

IT'S ALL IN THE RHYTHM

Okay, so we know that aligning the rhythm of your people (behavioural styles) with the rhythm of your business (culture, operating rhythms and skills) results in peak performance. This is what gives your business an unfair advantage. Activating these two frameworks in your business means you won't risk falling into controlling, micromanaging behaviour because you'll trust the team to be able to not only do their job but go above and beyond.

For each peak performance principle, we've outlined some key focus points that ensure you've got the four behavioural styles (DISC) covered.

Culture

1. A clear focus on outcomes and results, aligned with vision, goals and how to get there (D).

2. There's a vibe of variety, adventure and fun (I).

3. Due diligence when it comes to fair and equal treatment and taking care of people along the way (S).

4. Standards are held in terms of quality and accuracy (C).

Operating Rhythms

1. Clarity on 'for what purpose' and outcomes when it comes to operating rhythms in the business (D).

2. Challenge status quo and stay creative in the 'how' of doing things (I).

3. Consistency with meetings and people touchpoints to fuel core need of certainty. Don't promise the world and then not deliver (S).

4. Documented clarity of expectations and KPIs for each role (C).

Skills

1. Align growth and development to outcomes and goals (D).

2. Celebrate milestones – large and small – along the way (I).

3. Take the time to support people where they're at. Pause and check in with your people regularly (S).

4. Give individuals the time and space to learn and grow in their preferred styles (C).

DOERS TO DECISION-MAKERS

You can have *the* best business strategy in place, but strategy doesn't create business growth on its own – it's brought to life through your people.

Without your people continuing to grow and perform, your business will stagnate.

Building an empowered, autonomous team is the only way you'll get to step back from your business and have those holidays we talked about. You know, those holidays where you can completely switch off?

If you're thinking, *But I don't have time to do any more than I already am!* remember it doesn't always have to be you doing the work. In fact, sometimes it's best if it's *not* you. When creating an autonomous environment, lean on your leaders and your team. Look at growing your leadership team, outsourcing or working with external consultants. Getting support and not doing it all on your own is the best and quickest way to turn your doers into decision-makers, giving you the freedom you crave. We have so many clients that look to us to support their leadership teams for this exact reason. They may not have the time or the skills to embed the peak performance principles or dive into the behavioural styles within their teams. However you do it, just do it. There are always reasons *why not*, so we encourage you to ask instead, "How can I?"

Seventy-six percent of people surveyed by McCrindle believe working in a business **that invests in their development and with leaders who coach and develop them will positively impact engagement and retention.** What this stat tells us is that most of your workforce will stay with you longer and be more engaged, happier humans *if* you invest in them.

If creating an environment that people love coming to work for isn't reason enough to invest time and resources in your people and culture, then put your commercial business hat on.

Investing in culture and people will save you money, reduce staff turnover, and increase productivity and output.

Upskilling your people empowers them to take the reins and move from being doers to decision-makers. Investing in their development through training, coaching and mentoring allows them to grow in confidence and become more skilled and reliable. **Eighty percent of people who are coached see an increase in their self-confidence**, and over **70% benefit from improved work performance**, **relationships** and more **effective communication** skills. And for you as the person investing time and money in the development of your people, it's handy to keep in mind that **86% of businesses recoup their investment on outsourcing coaching *plus some*.** Coaching is a hidden superpower for your business … for both your people and your bottom line.

If it feels impossible right now, remember one of the main reasons businesses fail is due to not training or upskilling people. Can you afford not to prioritise this?

Critical Alignment

Mark had read all the leadership books, referenced the leadership models and learnt about being the person you need to be for the team at a given time, whether it's the authoritarian, participative or any of the other leadership styles. He was the first to admit his own leadership style was more reactionary than anything else.

At the time, he believed that when you're faced with a problem, you respond only to the problem and when you see a gap you respond only to the gap. It was up to other people in the organisation to worry about the culture and structure.

Mark went along hoping he was doing a good job, hoping he was onto the things that mattered. But the reality was he was stuck in a reactionary world. If he had a problem, he solved the problem, as opposed to seeing the problem as only a symptom to prompt exploration of the root cause. This was Mark's go-to way of working until he was introduced to the principles of peak performance.

With these principles in his toolkit, Mark is now more aware of looking broader than just the gap or the problem in isolation. His awareness has grown and the days of an underlying feeling of panic the night before a day off that something could go wrong, has gone. He knows it will all be okay because his team is set up for success with the right procedures and checklists handed down from the exec team. Everyone is across the processes, has the skills and can lean into their natural strengths. The right focus on culture and operating rhythms is in place, everyone can trust they're doing the right thing and ticking the boxes because they're aligned with the big picture goals *and* the steps on how to get there.

It's also impacted the attitude of leaders in his team – instead of feeling the need to be defensive or arrogant in their stance, they are now guided by the culture plans. They know how they want to be perceived and what to do to stay on track.

Until he started empowering his team and tailoring his communication to their particular behavioural style, he didn't know what he didn't know. In his words, that was really unsettling. But these days, he knows that he doesn't have to have all the answers and while that's still somewhat unsettling, it's okay because he has the framework to find the best solution and outcome, which is empowering for all involved.

The truth is that people-issues generally stem from a failure at a cultural or structural level. If we put all our attention on people without considering the other dimensions, like skills and strengths, it's like throwing somebody in icy water and telling them to smile (and not in the fun ice-bath craze way). So, if you solve problems at a cultural and operating rhythm (structure) level, you'll see an immediate improvement in people and their ability to take action with purpose. What a smart way to bring healthy hustle into your business!

CHAPTER FIVE.

Time Freedom: Your Path to Time Freedom

BANNING THE B-WORD

As a leader with a big workload, James H was hustling but not getting the reward for it. He was working hard not smart and he needed to be healthier in his hustling. He used to believe he didn't have enough time. This belief brought up feelings of anxiety and resulted in him rushing everywhere, being disorganised and not having much structure in his workday. This was not only impacting his output at work, but it also had a flow-on effect to his personal brand as a leader. His professional and personal image were taking a hit, with people often saying, "You seem really stressed, what's going on?" And ultimately, his manager saying after yet another missed deadline, "I have to follow up on you quite a bit to get something done."

This feedback was like a dagger in the heart for James H, because he didn't want to let anyone down. He was dropping balls at a rapid pace in all areas of his life, and he didn't like it.

One day he walked into a coaching session feeling overwhelmed, stressed and not his best self. But instead of showing how he really felt, he put on a façade – look at me, I'm happy. I'm all good. I could sense something was off and immediately cut through the BS, which allowed James H the opportunity to go deeper into understanding why he felt overwhelmed and why he wasn't reaching out for help.

James H came to the realisation that he believed asking for help was showing vulnerability. He thought vulnerability was a sign of weakness and he feared that reaching out for help would make his manager think he wasn't good at his job. So, his default became *be busy*. Distract from the true problem that needed solving. The surface problem is rarely the real problem that's driving unresourceful behaviour. In this case, the problem wasn't that James H was too busy, it was that he was procrastinating on tasks he didn't enjoy. There was also an underlying fear of getting things wrong and what that would look like to his manager and peers. Ironically, the thing he feared most was happening and became the barrier to him finding a better way of working – a way that was better for his brand, his team and, let's face it, his sanity.

Busy is an easy word to hide behind. It's lost all meaning – think about it, when you ask someone, "How's your day?" what's the most common answer you get? "Busy!" Everyone is busy in this world. Everyone. And saying the word busy is not only lazy, it also lets you off the hook. You're telling yourself, "Oh, it's okay to miss that deadline, I'm just busy."

The switch flicked for James H when he banned the word 'busy' and changed his language to, "I will" or "I can" or even "I could." The subtleties of language and the words we use have a huge impact on how we go about our day-to-day. Replacing the word 'busy' in the internal dialogue you have with yourself is a powerful way to also break the cycle of busy. And the next time someone asks how your day is going, please, we beg you – come up with something more real than just answering with this overused word.

James H started using other techniques in addition to being aware of his language, like using his calendar to allocate time to the things he'd subconsciously been avoiding, and working on his mindset and beliefs about what a successful leader looks like. And over time, he saw evidence in his results, which gave him positive reinforcement. The work James H did in this space has led him to become a transformational leader who is more effective and gets better results for his efforts. It's incredible to see him in action and observe other leaders coming to him for advice on how he leads his team and manages his workday. His managers now refer to him as their 'set and forget child' because he's so reliable and there's no need to follow up with him. When it's with James H, it's taken care of. This is what his brand is now known for after he found the courage to confront the true drivers of his behaviour, leaned into the discomfort, and broke out of the busy trap that was holding him back.

YOU DON'T NEED ANOTHER TIME MANAGEMENT TOOL

In two and a half years, the number of search results on Google for 'how I can manage my time more effectively' has increased by almost 6 billion, going from 514 million in September 2021 to 6.37 billion in March 2024.

There's no doubt the number of ways to manage your time are endless, and it can be somewhat overwhelming. Based on the increase in google search results, the increase in resources available over the last couple of years is exponential (a 1,239% increase to be exact) and indicates a rise in demand, a yearning from people to find a better way of spending their time. Certainly, this matches the conversations we're having with business leaders in coaching, workshops and roundtable events.

And yet, **88% of working people procrastinate daily** and the **average worker spends 51% of every workday on low to no-value tasks**. With only **20% of people feeling their work is under control daily** we have to wonder, what does this all tell us? It tells us, you do not need another time management tool!

We're sure you've done the courses and read the books, but it doesn't matter what time management tool you have at your fingertips because *if* you don't work on your mindset and beliefs around time, nothing will change.

If you believe there's not enough time, there will never be enough time.

Our unconscious mind doesn't know the difference between truth and fiction, so what are you telling it? You can feed it resourceful (helpful) or unresourceful (hindering) beliefs.

Examples of unresourceful, hindering beliefs: *I never have enough time; I have to do everything myself; I can't [xyz] because*

I don't have time; I have no choice; I should have done more by now; I'll do that tonight/on the weekend/on my holidays.

Examples of resourceful, helpful beliefs: *There's always enough time; I always get through it; It always works out in the end; I trust I will find time for the important things; Time expands to meet my priorities; I am the master of my time.*

Whichever type of beliefs you have, the hindering or helpful kind, the more you'll either stay stuck, or move through your day with ease. Without consciously realising it, you're always on the lookout for evidence of these beliefs to be true, so be careful which path you subscribe to.

INTRODUCING THE DO-BE MODEL

There's a beautiful balance of embracing both the DO and the BE to maximise time and efficiency.

Looking at the Do-Be Model below, where do you feel you sit right now?

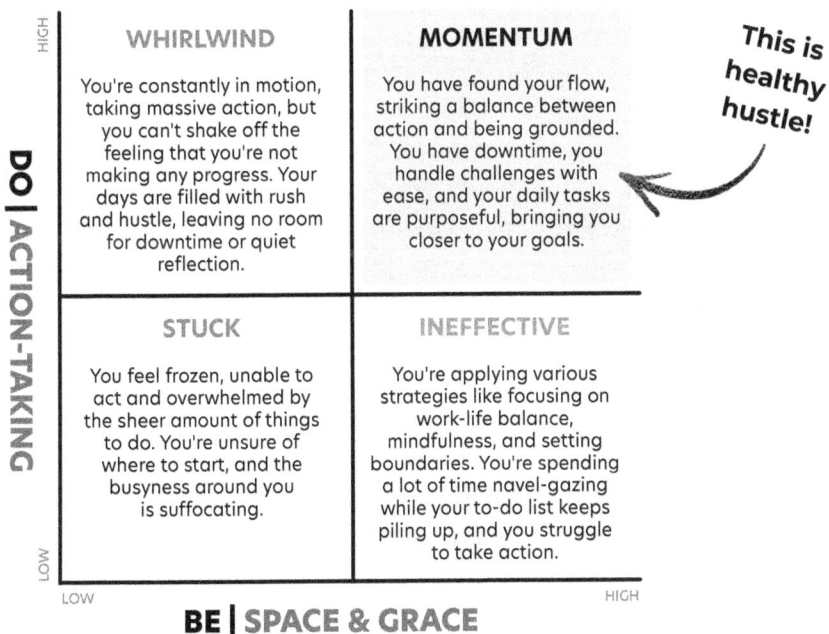

DO | ACTION-TAKING (vertical axis, HIGH to LOW)

WHIRLWIND
You're constantly in motion, taking massive action, but you can't shake off the feeling that you're not making any progress. Your days are filled with rush and hustle, leaving no room for downtime or quiet reflection.

MOMENTUM
You have found your flow, striking a balance between action and being grounded. You have downtime, you handle challenges with ease, and your daily tasks are purposeful, bringing you closer to your goals.

This is healthy hustle!

STUCK
You feel frozen, unable to act and overwhelmed by the sheer amount of things to do. You're unsure of where to start, and the busyness around you is suffocating.

INEFFECTIVE
You're applying various strategies like focusing on work-life balance, mindfulness, and setting boundaries. You're spending a lot of time navel-gazing while your to-do list keeps piling up, and you struggle to take action.

BE | SPACE & GRACE (horizontal axis, LOW to HIGH)

Do your inner and external dialogues (the words you say to yourself and to other people, respectively) align with where you are on the model? For example, if you find yourself always saying how busy you are or talking about lack of time (hindering beliefs), you'll likely find yourself in one of the left two quadrants – stuck or whirlwind.

We don't want to minimise the fact that you're a busy human with a lot going on. This conversation is about how you can minimise the risk of staying stuck in busy and maximising the chance for you to feel more space and grace in your life. Because it's possible!

BETTER USE OF TIME

Time as we know it today is a man-made concept and in this modern world of always being on, it's easy to monitor our time down to the millisecond without a thought. As Oliver Burkeman shares in his book *Four Thousand Weeks*:

> Before, time was just the medium in which life unfolded, the stuff that life was made of. Afterwards, once 'time' and 'life' had been separated in most people's minds, time became a *thing* that you *used* – and it's this shift that serves as the precondition for all the uniquely modern ways in which we struggle with time today.
>
> Once time is a resource to be used, you start to feel pressure, whether from external forces or from yourself, to use it well, and to berate yourself when you feel you've wasted it.
>
> When you're faced with too many demands, it's easy to assume the only answer must be to make *better use* of time, by becoming more efficient, driving yourself harder, or working for longer – as if you were a machine in the Industrial Revolution – instead of asking whether demands themselves might be unreasonable.

In the words of Mary Oliver (an American poet), *"Tell me, what is it you plan to do with your one wild and precious life?"*

Will you be swept into the whirlwind of hustle, constantly striving to make *better use* of your time and berate yourself when you feel you've wasted it? Or will you practise moving from being constantly busy to a place of living (see table on page 133) creating awareness of whether the demands you place on yourself are unreasonable.

Being stuck in the **busy** is when things feel chaotic and out of control, and you go through the days without any awareness of time passing you by. Ever get to the end of the day and think, *Woah, what happened?*

On the other hand, **living** is when things feel calm, somewhat under control, and like there's more flow, joy and presence in what you're doing. This is what healthy hustle is. You have moments of awareness throughout the day and it's no surprise when 5 pm comes around.

We often spend too much time worrying about the future, the unknown of what's to come, or stuck in regret, contemplation or wishing for the past. When we are living mindfully, we are present. Aware of the current moment and honouring the ways of time 'before' that Oliver Burkeman spoke about in *Four Thousand Weeks*. This allows us to beautifully let life and time to unfold together.

Imagine for a moment if you were in a space of *living* more than *busy*, what would be different in six months? What if your team were more present, deliberate in their actions. What would that look like?

✔ TOP TIP:

A quick way you can come back to *living* from *busy* is the Gratitude vs. Guilt exercise. You can only consciously focus on one of these emotions at a time so choosing something to focus on that you're grateful for will take you away from the chaos of busy and move you back to your present state of living.

Ask yourself, what could I be grateful for in this moment? Then ask yourself, what else? And what else? Depending on how deep you're stuck in your guilt will depend on how many times you ask yourself what you're grateful for.

Don't get stuck in overthinking here. The answers can be simple.

BUSY VS. LIVING

Of course, the reality of living in times where, as Canadian Prime Minister Justin Trudeau says, "The pace of change has never been this fast, yet it will never be this slow again," means you won't be able to avoid 'busy' all together.

The goal is to be aware enough to see if you're busy or living, focusing on the future or the past, so that you can get back to living your one wild and precious life in all its glory.

BUSY – Unhealthy Hustle

- Distractions
- Flustered
- Many tabs open on the computer and in your mind
- Guilt, always letting someone down
- Overusing the word 'should' – 'shoulding all over yourself'
- Overwhelm
- Never enough time
- Stressed
- Constant running
- No purpose in action, tasks for the sake of it
- Skipping urgent or important tasks
- Doing the loudest task
- No time for fun or joy
- Spinning wheels
- Every area of life feels rushed
- Groundhog day of getting stuff done

PAST | PRESENT | FUTURE

LIVING – Healthy Hustle

- Mindfulness
- Presence in the task at hand
- Joy and happiness in the day-to-day
- Connection
- Solutions
- Creativity
- Calm under pressure
- Time with loved ones outside of work
- Acceptance of what you can't control
- Working through tasks effectively
- Feeling a sense of accomplishment
- Pride in what's being achieved
- Clarity
- Purposeful action
- Values aligned
- Boundaries
- Relaxed and nourished

Where Are You Spending Your Time?

We all have 168 hours in a week to play with and are constantly prioritising the things we focus on, so let's get clear on where you're spending your time.

THE 168 TIME AUDIT

Grab a pen, paper and calculator (or get your math brain on) and create two columns, one for 'Big Rocks' and one for 'Hours per week' or you can play along below.

Fill in how many hours on average each week you spend in each of the areas below. If we've missed anything, feel free to add as you go. Then add up the total and do the reflections that follow.

Big Rocks	Hours per week
Meetings	
Travel (to and from office or between client meetings)	
Client delivery/client work	
Admin tasks	
Lunch and other breaks	

Sleeping	
Hobbies	
Exercise	
Time with family	
House responsibilities, such as cooking, cleaning, laundry	
Kid's sports	
Me time	
Self-care	
Other ...	
Total	___ - 168 = ___

Let's reflect.

- How many hours do you have left over in a week?

- Are there any Big Rocks you had zero hours for over the last week (such as breaks, me time, self-care)? What is this telling you?

- What was your initial response to some of the Big Rocks listed? Notice if there were feelings of resistance or dread, it's all feedback.

One of two things happen every time we do this exercise with clients.

Either, you have more time than you realised and this is a reality check that you could be spending more time on higher quality activities. Maybe Netflix and doom scrolling are taking up more time than you thought. Perhaps your belief around not having enough time isn't true and there's something else going on.

Or, you have less time than you realised and this is a different kind of reality check, showing you that you *literally* can't fit everything in without something giving (most often your health, sleep, wellbeing, zest for life).

Remember, we prioritise our time (unconsciously) based on what's important to us.

Answer these questions:

+ **What feedback are you being given looking at these results?**

+ **What are you spending the other x hours in a day on? Are they resourceful or unresourceful behaviours?**

+ **What would it look like if you swapped them out for things that fuel your soul?**

Check out Stephen Covey's Big Rocks video from the late 1980s. We absolutely love this video because not only is it entertaining to see the fashion – big hair and shoulder pads – it also shows that despite the almost six billion increase in Google results over the last few years, this is NOT a new problem!

Watch the Stephen Covey Big Rocks video

www.nickymiklos.com/book-resources

TIME FREEDOM

If you're not happy with the answers of your 168 Time Audit, instead of giving yourself a hard time, get curious and peek behind the curtain as to why you're doing what you're doing. What's the driving force behind the behaviour, because we're telling you right now, it's not laziness! There's always a reason. Things like:

- Core needs aren't being met and so you're striving to meet them in other ways.
- Pushing yourself too much and then not having any energy on the weekends.

- Unhappy in certain areas of your life or business, prompting avoidance strategies.
- Having a feeling of scarcity or fear, which can be debilitating.
- Self-confidence has taken a hit and procrastination feels like the safe option.

Through uncovering the cause of the behaviour instead of beating yourself up about it, you can start the move from hustle to happy.

You'll never have more time, and the more you aim for more time, the further away it will feel. Reframing your expectations, views and beliefs on time is going to be the key to giving you the *feeling* of more time, which will be the thing that gives you more space and grace in your day.

It's not about *doing* more, rather it's about being aware of what you're telling yourself, and others around you, how you're showing up to 'busy' and how you're showing up to 'living'. All the while giving yourself a regular reality check and clarity on where you're spending your time and why.

Remember time freedom can't happen without having smart growth in your business. Use the tools outlined so far, like planning for and getting clarity on your direction in business and life (True North Framework, Chapter 3), and uncovering the natural behavioural styles in your team (Chapter 4). Move from guilt to gratitude as well as looking at how you and the team are prioritising activities to help move the dial with your weekly, monthly, quarterly and yearly progress (PoP, Monthly Milestones, Five-to-Thrive, Chapter 3). Embrace the principles of people leadership with the peak performance principles (Chapter 4) to have an empowered, autonomous team. Applying all of these models and frameworks will help free you up, give you space. Even if you don't want to grow your business, you will benefit greatly from applying this in your business as you can focus then on prioritising life.

By not only focusing on vanity numbers like sales and turnover and focusing equally on profit, you'll have more cashflow to invest in your team. This will help upskill them to become decision-makers, not just doers, allowing you to be less hands on. Instead of winging it throughout the day, having clarity on everyone's top tasks for the week above and beyond business as usual will make sure you're achieving your Wildly Important Goals. Having proactive sales strategies and systems (Chapter 3 - Bonus Chapter) in place will create greater efficiencies in your team and allow everyone in your team to perform as well as your top performers. All of these things are going to be the key to building a team that steps up, so you can step back and choose where you're spending your time. Hello healthy hustle!

The Cause of Collapse

On 6 April 2007, Arianna Huffington was at home doing her typical day-in-the-office tasks when she collapsed and woke up to find herself lying in a pool of blood. She'd passed out and hit her head, cutting her eye and breaking her cheekbone on the way down. Not knowing what had caused the event, Arianna went from doctor to doctor and sought medical advice, fearing the worst. The diagnosis was conclusive. The cause of the collapse was due to exhaustion, stress and lack of sleep. Working eighteen-hour days, seven days a week will do that. The push, grind, hustle, and go-go-go of dealing with rapid growth in her business was literally sucking the life out of her.

As the co-founder of *Huffington Post*, founder and CEO of Thrive Global and bestselling author, Arianna is one of *Forbes* most powerful women and, at the time, she was being named in *Time Magazine*'s world's 100 most influential people.

The irony is not lost, Arianna being named one of *Time Magazine*'s most influential people at *the same time* she collapses with exhaustion and unwittingly causes physical harm to her own wellbeing from being driven and working hard. Remember when we mentioned we have a duty of care?!

This was a big wakeup call for Arianna who decided to create some changes in her life, including writing two bestselling books (*Thrive* and *The Sleep Revolution* – both of which we highly recommend), launching Thrive Global, and starting a very global and public conversation about redefining success. The big message is to value wellbeing, wisdom, giving and wonder just as much as we value money, power and influence. I remember reading this in her book *Thrive* not long after my own experience with exhaustion and burnout and thinking, *Finally!*

Finally, there's a different point of view being brought to the table when it comes to figuring out what success looks like. A person who is respected and highly influential was smashing the norms of the traditional measures of success. This was a turning point to be able to bring these principles into corporate business and then later to small-medium businesses.

When we think about smart growth and doing business on your own terms, we think about Arianna's story and the importance of a holistic view (and measure) of success. Breaking free of the busy trap and leading your people to time freedom means you need to redefine not only what *success* means to you, but also your beliefs around *time*. Because time is the gatekeeper holding you back from, or welcoming you to, what's next for you and your business.

PART THREE.

The Road Ahead

Working smart is no longer a luxury, it's a necessity. Gone are the days of winging it. Understanding the difference between what got you here, and what will get you there, is the key to unlocking your next frontier of growth. These pages so far have given you strategies, tips and stories of inspiration from others who have been at their growth set point and are now embracing these healthy hustle principles. But if you don't do anything with them, then this will have been a good read and that's about it. Or it will be yet another book for the pile of half-read books that you'll get to actioning one day. We want to break that cycle and make it easy for you to install the strategies we've shared.

We also want you to know exactly what phase of smart growth you're in right now. When you know where you are, you can have a choice in where you're headed. At the moment, you're in either Crisis, Build, Growth or Momentum mode. Perhaps you're at your own growth set point and are on a crescendo of change. You've probably heard the phrase 'knowledge is power'. This might be controversial, but we disagree. A better phrase would be 'knowledge is *potential* power'. It's what you do with that knowledge that matters. You can read, listen to or watch the most informative resources, but if you don't do anything with them, so what? It's not the knowledge that makes you powerful, it's the implementation of that knowledge that gets you where you want to go. As Stephen Covey said so well "To know and not to do, is not to know."

In the following chapter we're going to show you the road to smart business growth and you'll get to identify which phase you're in right now. You'll also get access to additional resources to plan your profit, get proactive with your sales activities and be consistent with your team communication. You can jump in and grab these straight away at www.nickymiklos.com/book-resources.

CHAPTER SIX.

Your Smart Growth Blueprint

FROM CRISIS TO MOMENTUM

CRISIS	BUILD	GROWTH	MOMENTUM
Running off fumes, focusing only on the urgent (or the loudest thing getting your attention).	You have better clarity on the business goals and vision, but your team aren't working autonomously.	There's a danger of a 'good enough' mentality, which can cause a plateau or even a decline in the business.	This is where it's at! There's consistent planning, equal focus on sales + profit and the team are empowered and autonomous.

Psst – it's no coincidence that the DO-BE Model and the four phases of smart growth in business, end up in momentum. Momentum is a key part of healthy hustle!

There are typically four life-cycle phases that a business falls into at any given time. For you to achieve healthy hustle, you need to have awareness of what phase you're in, and how to move through, ultimately, to momentum. It's not set and forget as you move in and out of multiple phases during the lifespan of your business. There will be times when different areas of your business will fall into different areas of smart business growth. It's worthwhile checking in on this scale regularly to see which way you're moving and where you're headed (crisis to momentum or momentum to crisis). Whatever phase you find yourself in, you're able to maintain or change depending on your people, systems and culture.

Phase 1: Crisis

When you're in crisis mode, you're running off fumes, focusing only on the urgent (or the loudest thing getting your attention) and doing what you need to get through the day. It's bloody exhausting and very likely you're feeling adrift, without direction and in the whirlwind of busy. Chances are you don't have a clear plan for the next ninety days and if you do, you might've lost it under your growing pile of to-dos.

Your business feels chaotic (even if it is making great sales) and living on Juggle Street is real. Being all things to all people, you might be feeling frustrated with the lack of autonomy and communication within the team. We'd hazard a guess that you're not feeling very supported and are deeply stuck in the busy trap (seriously, is this why you went into business?!).

We're going to give you some tough love, because the hard truth is that you can't keep going the way you are. Not only is it not enjoyable, and not what you went into business for in the first place, it's simply not sustainable for the long term and you will not achieve healthy hustle by staying here.

Phase 2: Build

In build mode you're still spinning the wheels with what needs to be done and juggling all the balls. Some days it might feel like you're holding on by the skin of your teeth but on others you're starting to see the light at the end of the tunnel. With everything going on around you it's up to you to keep it all together for your team, your family, your clients, and it can feel like a solo mission at times. You've got great ideas, but limited time to execute them, which makes you feel like you're capping the potential of the business and there's always more you could be doing.

You have better clarity on the business goals and vision than in crisis mode, but it hasn't translated to your team being empowered to work autonomously in striving towards the same outcomes as you. In build mode you're likely to be experiencing great sales but inconsistent profit. Communication among the team and even with you can be hit and miss. We often see business owners use the 'bury your head in the sand' strategy when they're in build mode. Because even though it feels hard right now, it feels even harder to think about doing things differently than to keep going the way you are.

Phase 3:
Growth

Growth mode indicates there are some great things happening in your business when it comes to clarity of outcomes and planning, as well as sales and profit. BUT you still feel like you're juggling all the balls and the consistency with your team can be wobbly. Despite the external challenges and market impact, your business is growing and you have some good systems in place to generate new business and increase profit.

In growth mode there's a danger of a 'good enough' mentality, which can cause a plateau or even a decline in the business. The problem is you've got so many spinning plates you're afraid if you take your eye off one of them, the whole thing will topple.

It's highly likely your business success is reliant on you being in the business. This could mean you can't remember the last time you took a holiday, or at least one where you completely switched off and were uncontactable by clients or the team.

Phase 4:
Momentum

This is where it's at! There's consistent planning – both long-term and short-term pulse checks – equal attention to sales and profit, and your team is empowered and autonomous. You and your leaders can step back with minimal-to-no impact on the business. You're in flow with a beautiful balance between doing (action) and being (space and grace) and the results are showing in your business and in your personal life.

When you hit momentum, the first thing to do is pause. Take the time to acknowledge and celebrate this result. Reflect on how you got here ... what is the secret to your success? What are the success strategies you want to continue with and, equally important, what's not working? What do you need to keep and let go of to get you to your next growth curve?

No business is 100% consistent 100% of the time. And this is why we call it momentum mode. Success is replicable – once we know the formula it can be repeated. Slowing down to speed up and gain momentum is key for your next frontier of growth.

Let's get practical so you can see what phase you're in right now. Look at the questions below and rate yourself 1 to 10 in each area.

Questions

1. How are you feeling about your business right now?

   1 = stuck, 10 = on fire

2. Do you have a plan for the next 90 days?

   1 = no, 10 = yes

3. Are you satisfied with the level of profit in your business?

   1 = no, 10 = yes

4. Do you have a system in place to generate new business opportunities?

1 = stuck, 10 = on fire

1 — 2 — 3 — 4 — 5 — 6 — 7 — 8 — 9 — 10

5. Are your team members working autonomously?

1 = no, 10 = yes

1 — 2 — 3 — 4 — 5 — 6 — 7 — 8 — 9 — 10

6. Is there effective communication both within the team and with you?

1 = no, 10 = yes

1 — 2 — 3 — 4 — 5 — 6 — 7 — 8 — 9 — 10

7. Do you feel supported in your role as a business owner or leader?

1 = no, 10 = yes

1 — 2 — 3 — 4 — 5 — 6 — 7 — 8 — 9 — 10

Your score card:

If you scored between 0 and 15, you're in **Crisis** mode.	If you scored between 46 and 64, you're in **Growth** mode.
If you scored between 16 and 45, you're in **Build** mode.	If you scored between 65 and 70, you're in **Momentum** mode.

BEST KEPT SECRETS

Having been in business for over twenty-one years, Michelle and Douglas have experienced all the phases of smart business growth at one time or another. They not only know that business growth isn't linear, they also embrace that it's not linear and prepare for it. At any given time, certain parts of your business could be in momentum while other areas are in crisis or build mode. Success comes down to how well you manage the experience for your leaders and team.

Michelle shares it's easy to look at your success and think, *Oh, we're at momentum and everything's really good.* Then thoughts sneak in of, *This can't last, something's going to change. If we're going to be the leader in our market, we need to keep ahead. What can we do that's more than what we're already doing so we're not caught out?* But if you do something that isn't well thought out and well communicated, it's easy for the business to quickly flip back to crisis mode.

As owners, Michelle and Douglas often discuss between themselves what changes they want to make in the business to stay in growth and momentum. In one instance, they'd nutted out a brilliant plan, gotten the strategy sorted, talked about talking to the leaders and were ready to move on it. They pulled the trigger, it was go time! Only then they realised ... they'd actually forgotten to talk to anyone else about their brilliant idea. It was the best kept secret in the business to date.

This was a big business lesson for Michelle and Douglas because when they eventually talked to their leaders, the team felt blindsided and didn't understand why the change was happening. The benefits weren't clear to them and they felt like they were just being asked to do more. This thing that Michelle and Douglas believed in and thought would take the business to their next frontier of growth, had become something that no one else believed in and it was pushed back against.

It all came down to communication. Michelle uses an analogy of a 'communication ball'. It's like an AFL football, you bounce it, and it could go in any direction. And if you're not careful and pay attention to how you hold and throw the ball, it could bounce in a completely different direction than you wanted it to. It might get away from you before you realise it. Unlike any other ball, it won't necessarily bounce straight back up for us to catch before it causes unwanted chaos elsewhere.

To get back on track in these times, Michelle and Douglas double down on the rhythms in their business. Remember we talked about rhythms of your people (understanding the four behavioural styles) aligning with the rhythms of your business (culture, operating rhythms and skills). For Michelle and Douglas, this includes consistent management meetings, and 90-day quarterly planning that's then checked in on monthly and weekly to stay on track. These rhythms keep communication lines open between everybody and make sure the bouncing ball is going in the right direction. It also helps everyone understand where they're going, and why and what they're trying to achieve.

Michelle's advice? If your leaders haven't been brought on the journey, stop and take the time to bring them on board. They're a critical piece of the puzzle to get the business to continuous growth and momentum. You're not an ER surgeon making lifesaving decisions here. You don't need to make an immediate decision in a matter of seconds because someone's life depends on it. This is business, unless you're at a point where this decision is going to mean the doors staying open or closed (in which case, you've already missed some pivotal points along the way), there's always time to just slow down. Even if it's for an hour to have a conversation with your team and check in with what the plan is.

You might also be surprised by what comes out of involving your leadership team. There's a reason they're in your business and they'll have different perspectives and points of view to contribute. Especially if you've nurtured their natural behaviour styles and applied the peak performance principles.

TAKE CONTROL OF YOUR DESTINY

Deeply engrained beliefs are why it's damn hard to break some cycles. They've become inherently embedded over how many years? Seriously think about this. How many years have you been working? Not just in business but since you very first started working probably at fourteen years and nine months. I know I was counting down the days to be able to make my own money and was stoked to start working at Sawtell Seaside Seafoods – my first job (if you don't count the two times I did the early morning paper round, yep, not a part of the 5 am Club back then either!).

Truth be told, you've been unconsciously creating beliefs about what success looks like even before you started that first job in the fish and chip shop (or Red Rooster, Coles, the bowls club). Subconsciously taking in the beliefs of your role models about hard work, money and success.

All the events you've experienced in your life have created and continue to integrate your beliefs. As humans we're wired to always be looking for evidence for our beliefs to be true.

Your brain's reticular activating system (RAS) is like a homing beacon looking out for the things that have been flagged as important.

I was beyond excited when I got my first MINI Cooper, it was red, and it was awesome. But then I started seeing red MINIs everywhere. Was it because there were suddenly more on the road now? Nope. They were always there. Ever noticed when you have someone close to you who's pregnant, you start seeing pregnant women everywhere? Are there suddenly more pregnant women around? Probs not, you're seeing them more because they're now important enough to consciously notice. That's your RAS in action.

When you consider the road to smart growth, what types of beliefs do you think lie in each area?

DOWN THE RABBIT HOLE

We have 11 million bits of information per second being thrown at our brain to process. We can't possibly bring all of this into our conscious awareness, or our mind would explode (okay, so that's not a technically accurate description, but you get the idea). Suffice to say, it's too much to process and so we filter the information down to around fifty bits – or seven to nine chunks of information. That means there's a heck of a lot going on around us that we don't even notice. How does our internal filtering system know what to prioritise into those seven to nine chunks? It looks for evidence for our beliefs to be true and for what aligns with our values. It's the reason the famous saying 'what you focus on is what you get' rings true.

Notice on those days when you get out of the wrong side of bed and you just know it's going to be an uphill battle? Your homing beacon is set on a channel to seek out all the reasons that day sucks and there's even a sense of satisfaction in being proven right as all the drama unfolds. I can honestly say since I became aware of my RAS, I've not gotten out of the wrong side of the bed. Not because I haven't had days that had a sh*t show element to them, but because I'm aware of not setting my subconscious search channel (the RAS) to go looking for evidence of 'wrong side of the bed'. It minimises (not removes) what I notice around me relevant to this.

We're curious, what channel is yours set to?

Are you looking for evidence to prove that hustling hard is the only way to succeed?

To justify why you're stuck in crisis or build mode and all the reasons why you can't move out of it. What came up for you when you did the time exercise (the 168 Time Audit). Did you hear yourself saying *yes but...*, *that's fine for you...*, *it's different for me* ... these are the clues to show you what your RAS is looking for!

Your beliefs are the foundations of the cycles that need to be broken. You *can* change your beliefs. This means changing your beliefs can change your business and your life. No joke! How long it takes is dependent on things like how ready you are to create change, how deeply engrained the belief is, and your ability to find evidence points for your new beliefs. You can't remove a belief without replacing it with something else, otherwise the old crappy belief will continue to sneak back in.

Here are common unresourceful beliefs we see from busy business owners and leaders; how many do you resonate with?

- I just need to get through x project/period/delivery and then I'll be able to [insert ideal scenario like leave work on time, have a holiday].

- We just have to work harder and put in extra hours to get through it.

- I've got to work outside of working hours to get anything done.

- There's not enough time in the day.

- It needs to be perfect.

- It's easier if I do it myself.

Remember the **7 Business Truths** at the beginning of the book? Imagine if they inspired your new beliefs and you could kick those crappy old ones to the curb – what would that look like for you? For your team?

Here's seven beliefs to try on and see how they feel:

1. I have a killer, successful business *and* still have a life.

2. My team and I work smart, with ease, and still get results.

3. Having holidays is our badge of honour.

4. I set the rules of my business.

5. My team is an empowered team and they step up so I can step back.

6. My business is thriving, my team is thriving and I'm thriving too!

7. I hustle in a healthy way.

✔ **TOP TIP:**

Don't be surprised if these new beliefs feel a bit uncomfortable at first, it's like trying on a new pair of shoes. Sometimes you've got to walk around in them for a bit before they start to feel more comfy.

WORKING SMARTER IS NO LONGER A LUXURY

It's true ... cost of living has gone up.

It's true ... businesses are facing budget challenges.

It's true ... work feels harder than ever.

It's true ... you're having to do more with less.

It's true ... it's highly competitive out there.

It's true ... your people are frustrated and disengaged.

What's also true is ... **you're still leading this company.**

What's also true is ... **you still have a vision.**

What's also true is ... **you still want to grow the business.**

Business owners often tell us they want to be in momentum mode. But it's important you know there's a downside. You're not as needed; the business will run smoothly in your absence so there's not as many opportunities to sweep in and save the day. Results aren't solely reliant on you, and you have to let go – even if people do things a different way to you, you've got to find a way to be okay with that. These downsides might sound great. In theory they always do. In practice it can be a bit more challenging because you're used to being at the centre of it all, making sure things happen. This being needed in the business can be addictive and it's one of the main reasons you're the bottleneck of your business.

In 2015 Amy Morin (psychotherapist and international bestselling mental strength author) published an article in *Forbes* stating that, "Addiction is characterized by compulsive engagement in rewarding stimuli, despite the adverse consequences." A person with a gambling addiction will keep going back to the pokies even if they're in debt. The sporadic wins are enough positive reinforcement to keep them going.

Even though working long hours could lead to social consequences, like friction in your marriage or chronic stress, you just can't help yourself. *I'll just finish that one last email, make one more phone call, send off that final brief for the day.*

The 'one more' ... always leaves you wanting more.

Behavioural addictions include psychological dependence and some of the warning signs of an entrepreneurial addiction are:

- **Obsessive thoughts** (constantly thinking about your business – getting new clients, introducing new products, the next onboarding round...).
- **Withdrawal** (once that big pitch or project is done withdrawal symptoms can occur, including boredom, depression, anxiety, a feeling of 'coming down').
- **Self-worth problems** (never acknowledging how far you've come or celebrating your successes before searching for the next big thing will impact your self-worth, it's never enough).
- **Increased tolerance** to your substance of choice, in this case unhealthy ways of working (the long hours, no lunch breaks or lack of sleep become the normal way to function).
- **Neglect** (other areas of life come second and are neglected – your health, family, time for you, hobbies, sleep).
- **Negative outcomes** (continuing your way of working despite the negative effects on your health, relationships, life).

We wonder how much you relate to these signs of addiction. It might be a sobering thought to realise that you've unintentionally become addicted to your business. We know for sure that at different times we can relate to some (or, in the past, all) of these signs. This isn't about dumping a bucket of sick on ourselves. It's about awareness. With awareness you can take the first step to recovery. Your beliefs also feed into these signs of being addicted to your work. You might've learnt somewhere along the way that the only way to be successful is to work long hours, or that to miss your lunch break showed you were serious about your job. You might've seen your parents sacrifice time at the dinner table for their work.

It's all connected, and if we can change our beliefs, we change our habits and behaviours. As a business leader, it's also important to consider what example you're setting for the people around you. How are you impacting the beliefs your team are creating and embedding in their everyday lives? Remember actions speak louder than words.

I'm Out

Simon started his engineering business back in 1992, at the tail end of a recession. Since then, he's managed to navigate four economic cycles and, apart from the occasional doubt about whether any work would come in during the early days, the business has continued to be successful, as measured by how profitable the business has remained.

The model and the principles that he started the business with have barely altered since. As the business has grown, it's been a scaling process based on the same foundations. There have been challenges along the way, but they've mainly been people challenges, staff challenges and fitting the building blocks of the mission and vision together so that they attract the right team.

There was a time in the early 2000s when Simon bought into a finance franchise business. He fell into the behavioural addictions of an entrepreneur and became very obsessed with this new shiny thing. He was flying around the country speaking, getting lots of dopamine hits from standing up in front of a thousand people and presenting, getting laughs from engaged audiences.

He describes himself in this experience as having zero principles and zero knowledge. He was relying on others, learning and doing. He was a seminar presenter, an options trader and an educator. He was doing this on the side and running his engineering practice. The engineering practice kept going because the right systems were in place. But in the business that he was trying to create, he never made a dollar. Even though the experience gave him so much knowledge that he was able to apply in all areas of business and life, he remembers being obsessive, totally driven and full of ego.

As an absent parent, the impact on his family was hugely negative. He physically wasn't there for a period of time. He was flying out on Sunday night and arriving home on Friday night. With a two-year-old and a new baby, the load was heavily left on his wife. And that was the cost of his entrepreneurial addictions.

Simon's moment of epiphany was that he was going to lose everything that mattered the most to him if he kept going down that path. That was the day he got in the car and drove for four hours to his business partners with all the documentation in hand and said, "You can have it all back. See you later." He didn't fight anybody, didn't put the blame on anyone else. He just said, "I'm out," and left. Simon knew this was the best outcome because suddenly he freed up all that time to focus on what really mattered most.

Conclusion

Remember Michelle and Douglas from Chapter 6? They had nurtured their company from a fledgling idea into a robust enterprise with a dedicated team of thirty-five and one day they found themselves asking each other – what next? What if we lived overseas for a year – could the business survive if we stepped away for that long? Despite the practicalities of running the business and raising children, the notion lingered, growing stronger each day.

Determined to explore this wild idea, they decided to test its feasibility. Michelle and Douglas listed every possible roadblock: logistics of travel, schooling, running the business remotely. They scrutinised each one, expecting to find an insurmountable obstacle.

"We think we might do it. And then, of course, the brain says, 'No, that's ridiculous, you can't do that. You've got a business, you've got kids.' And so what we did with that was we said, 'Okay, what's smart to do here is to find the absolute.' We agree, it's a silly idea. You don't take your kids out of school and leave your business for twelve months. That's absolutely ridiculous. So let's go and find the big roadblock that's gonna stop us, because at some point later, we're going to look back and say I wonder if we'd done that... and if we can say, 'Do you know what, it wasn't possible because we couldn't get a visa or we couldn't run the business, or we couldn't get the kids into whatever it was going to be.' Once we found that big roadblock that was insurmountable, we could say, 'Excellent, we don't need to do it.' Well, every potential roadblock fell away. And so then we're left with ... we have to do this. We have to do this now or be prepared to live with the wondering. So, we did it."

Months of meticulous planning followed. They prepared their team for the challenge ahead, instilling confidence and autonomy in each person. Their message to the team? "You can't break the business. Make the best decisions you know how to make, and we'll evaluate afterwards."

The day finally came, and with a mixture of excitement and trepidation, Michelle, Douglas and their children boarded a plane to Spain. They settled in Granada, a city rich in culture and history, nestled at the foothills of the Sierra Nevada mountains. Every day was a new adventure – exploring winding cobblestone streets, tasting exotic foods and immersing themselves in the vibrant local life.

Back home, their business continued to thrive. The team, empowered by the trust Michelle and Douglas had placed in them, navigated the challenges with remarkable resilience. They handled inquiries, managed projects and made decisions, all while growing stronger and more cohesive.

Michelle and Douglas stayed connected with the team through regular check-ins but their involvement was minimal – just enough to ensure everything was on track. The time difference meant that often issues resolved before they had a chance to respond. It was a lesson in patience and trust, proving that sometimes the best action is to step back and let others step up.

"We lived in Granada in the south of Spain for twelve months. We made lovely friends, we travelled, we experienced, and really enjoyed that. Douglas did two trips back to Australia to check in on the business and we probably did about eight hours a week between us remotely checking in and keeping things going. The business grew in that period of time."

Their year in Spain was transformative. Michelle and her family grew closer, relying on each other in a foreign land where they had no one else. The business, too, evolved, benefiting from the autonomy and confidence built within the team.

As the year drew to a close, Michelle and Douglas returned home, enriched by their experiences. They were greeted by a team that had not only survived but thrived in their absence. The business had grown, and so had everyone involved.

Reflecting on their journey, Michelle realised that their adventure had been about more than just living abroad. It was a testament to the strength of their vision, the power of trust and the importance of embracing the unknown. It was a reminder that sometimes the wildest ideas can lead to the most profound growth, both personally and professionally. And that when you have the systems and frameworks set up in your business, it is absolutely 100% possible for you as the business owner to step back. This is the truest example of empowering your team to step up, so that you can step back and choose your level of involvement in the business.

If chaos is driving poor decisions, you've likely at one time questioned – is it all worth it? Or is it easier to just throw it all in. But you've worked so hard and come so far and this is your crossroads, your growth set point waiting for your next move. Your version of going to Spain for twelve months – what is this for you? What would you do with the precious time that would be gifted back to you? Untethering yourself from the business and closing the gap between *why* you went into business and your current *reality* is doable. Just look at what Michelle and Douglas along with James, Jodie, Christine and so many others have achieved.

This book is about winning in business and life. And just as importantly not winning *at all costs*... and especially not at your cost. Yes, your business feels chaotic, but now that you know how to spot the difference between beautiful and destructive chaos, you know how to identify if it's functional or dysfunctional and what to do about it. You've been equipped with the formulas and tools to make sure you and your team are experiencing positive stress, steering clear from negative and chronic stress. Too often, smart individuals like yourself become statistics of burnout or chronic stress-related illnesses. With these resources at your fingertips, you can mitigate the risks and maintain your wellbeing and that of the people around you. You can find your version of a year in Spain to aspire to.

As you now know, the only way to free yourself (and your team) from the busy trap is via smart growth and peak performance principles. The reason 'work–life balance' hasn't worked before is potentially because you haven't embedded these frameworks into your business (or maybe you had some, but not consistently). Despite your best efforts, and without realising it, you've set yourself up to fail because without these tools, systems and models there is no way that a business owner or leader can step back. Without these principles in practice, no matter what you do, you'll always be needed in the day-to-day.

The Thrive Business Model (Page 65) helps you lay the foundations, optimise for growth and accelerate results in business, leading you to healthy hustle. Remember: strategy alone will not create sustainable business growth, it's the people that bring it to life.

It's time to stop being the bottleneck in your business, get unaddicted to work, embrace beautiful chaos and confidently empower your team. This is the path to get back to living.

There are proven examples and frameworks weaved throughout this book that will elevate your business growth and give you time back. The two are not mutually exclusive.

After decades of working with businesses, either helping them with their advertising, facilitating performance and sales coaching, or doing leadership consulting and training, we have seen the resistance to change at the detriment of the business owner and the overall business and teams. Those that are left behind stay stuck due to fear or being 'too busy' to do things differently.

We implore you: do something, even one thing, with what you've learnt in this book. Don't let this be a wasted opportunity. This book isn't going to magically fix your problems and do the work for you (if only, how great would that be!) It's the road map to follow as you choose your own adventure. So, what will it be? Keep going as is, bury your head in the sand or be courageous enough to do something different?

CHOOSE YOUR OWN ADVENTURE MAP

To revisit key tools, themes, ideas and resources in this book, look at the below area you want to revisit and simply get started.

Work with Nicky

If reading Healthy Hustle has inspired you to rethink how you work, lead, and grow, now is the perfect time to take the next step.

I help business owners and leadership teams turn ideas into action. Together, we'll create the clarity, systems, and leadership capability you need to:

- Activate sustainable, consistent sales growth
- Shift from reactive, day-to-day firefighting to proactive, strategic growth
- Build confident leaders who drive results without burning out
- Create a business (and team) that thrives, even when you step away

Whether you're looking for a keynote speaker to inspire an audience, a targeted workshop to solve a specific challenge, or ongoing coaching to transform your sales and leadership culture, I'll help you find your own sweet spot of healthy hustle and leverage smart growth for sustainable success.

Let's make your next chapter your best yet.

Visit **nickymiklos.com** to explore services, enquire about speaking, or start a conversation about how we can work together.

The best ways to contact Nicky are:

Email: hello@nickymiklos.com
Website: www.nickymiklos.com
LinkedIn Nicky: https://www.linkedin.com/in/connectwithnicky/
(or Nicky Miklós)

Sources

Introduction

Insights with Joe Pane the Podcast (2023) E82. *This ONE THING can massively impact 2023* https://www.joepane.com.au/blog/this-one-thing-can-massively-impact-2023

Part 1

Marshall Goldsmith (2007) *What got you here wont get you there; How Successful People Become Even More Successful!* Hachette Books.

Chapter 1

Elizabeth Gilbert (2007) *Eat, Pray Love* Riverhead Books

Deloitte (2018) *Workplace Burnout Survey: Burnout without borders* https://www2.deloitte.com/us/en/pages/about-deloitte/articles/burnout-survey.html

Gallup (2018) *Employee Burnout, Part 1: The 5 Main Causes* https://www.gallup.com/workplace/237059/employee-burnout-part-main-causes.aspx

Lawpath (2024) *Statistics on Small Businesses in Australia: 2024 Update* https://lawpath.com.au/blog/small-businesses-statistics

Clarify Capital (2024) *What Percentage of Businesses Fail? [2024]* https://clarifycapital.com/blog/what-percentage-of-businesses-fail

Chapter 2

Inside Small Business (2022) *Small-business owners eschewing their annual leave* https://insidesmallbusiness.com.au/latest-news/small-business-owners-eschewing-their-annual-leave

Roy Morgan (2023) *Australians have 200 million days of annual leave due* https://www.roymorgan.com/findings/australians-have-200-million-days-of-annual-leave-due

On Deck (2022) *Time for a break: 1 in 3 small business owners take less than 2 weeks leave annually* https://www.ondeck.com.au/press-releases/time-for-a-break-1-in-3-small-business-owners-take-less-than-2-weeks-leave-annually

Stanford Institute For Economic Policy Research (2013) *The Productivity Of Working Hours* By John Pencavel https://siepr.stanford.edu/publications/working-paper/productivity-working-hours

Chapter 3

Banner Health (2022) *Good Stress vs. Bad Stress: How Can You Tell the Difference?* https://www.bannerhealth.com/healthcareblog/teach-me/bad-stress-vs-good-stress-how-can-i-tell-the-difference

Harvard Medical School (2024) *Understanding the stress response* https://www.health.harvard.edu/staying-healthy/understanding-the-stress-response

The Medical Journal of Australia (2019) *The financial cost of intensive care in Australia: a multicentre registry study* https://www.mja.com.au/journal/2019/211/7/financial-cost-intensive-care-australia-multicentre-registry-study

NIB Health Funds (2021) *The impact of stress in Australia* https://www.nib.com.au/the-checkup/impact-of-stress-in-australia

CFAH (2024) *Stress in the Workplace Statistics* (2024 Update) https://cfah.org/workplace-stress-statistics/#references

Harrisons *How to calculate your employee turnover costs* https://hhr.com.au/costs-of-employee-turnover

Australian Bureau of Statistics (2024) *Average Weekly Earnings, Australia* https://www.abs.gov.au/statistics/labour/earnings-and-working-conditions/average-weekly-earnings-australia/latest-release

WebMD (2024) *The Effects of Stress on Your Body* https://www.webmd.com/balance/stress-management/effects-of-stress-on-your-body

Harvard Business Review (2019) *What Makes Some People More Productive Than Others* https://hbr.org/2019/03/what-makes-some-people-more-productive-than-others

Stephen R Covey (1996) *First Things First* Prentice Hall

Salesforce (2015) *Quest for Growth Report* Salesforce

Thrive My Way (2023) *Important Burnout Stats 2024 [Trends and Facts to Know]* https://thrivemyway.com/burnout-stats/

Hubspot (2023) *HubSpot's 2024 State of Sales Report: How 1400+ Pros Will Navigate AI & Other Trends* https://blog.hubspot.com/sales/hubspot-sales-strategy-report

Forbes (2022) *Customer Retention Versus Customer Acquisition* https://www.forbes.com/councils/forbesbusinesscouncil/2022/12/12/customer-retention-versus-customer-acquisition/

Brevet (2014) *21 Mind-Blowing Sales Stats* https://blog.thebrevetgroup.com/21-mind-blowing-sales-stats

Saleslion (2023) *91% of customers say they'd give referrals. Only 11% of salespeople ask for referrals* https://saleslion.io/sales-statistics/91-of-customers-say-theyd-give-referrals-only-11-of-salespeople-ask-for-referrals/

LXA (2023) *Sales and Marketing Alignment: Stats and Trends for 2023* https://www.lxahub.com/stories/sales-and-marketing-alignment-stats-and-trends-2023

Sales Ninja Training (2023) *The Importance of Sales Training: Boosting Your Sales Team's Success* https://www.linkedin.com/pulse/importance-sales-training-boosting-your-teams-success/

Chapter 4

HR Profiling Solutions (2024) *What behavioural theories underpin Extended DISC®?* https://hrprofilingsolutions.com.au/tools/disc-profiles/

DISC Insights *William Marston, Father of DISC* https://discinsights.com/pages/william-marston-disc

McCrindle (2022) *Shaping the future culture infographic* https://mccrindle.com.au/resource/infographic/shaping-thriving-culture-infographic/

Forbes (2021) *Is Micromanaging A Form Of Bullying? Here Are 3 Things You Should Know* https://www.forbes.com/sites/heidilynnekurter/2021/06/29/is-micromanaging-a-form-of-bullying-here-are-3-things-you-should-know/

Luisa Zhou (2024) *The Ultimate List of Life Coaching Statistics in 2024* https://luisazhou.com/blog/life-coaching-statistics/

REFERENCES

Chapter 5

Jobera (2024) *50+ Time Management Statistics, Trends and Facts [2024]* https://jobera.com/time-management-statistics/

Runn (2024) *Time Management Statistics: Understand Where Your Workday Goes* https://www.runn.io/blog/time-management-statistics

Oliver Burkeman (2022) *Four Thousand Weeks: Embrace your limits. Change your life. Make your four thousand weeks count* Vintage Arrow

Library of Congress *Poem 133: The Summer Day* https://www.loc.gov/programs/poetry-and-literature/poet-laureate/poet-laureate-projects/poetry-180/all-poems/item/poetry-180-133/the-summer-day/

World Economic Forum (2018) *Justin Trudeau's Davos address in full* https://www.weforum.org/agenda/2018/01/pm-keynote-remarks-for-world-economic-forum-2018/

Medium (2017) *10 Years Ago I Collapsed From Burnout and Exhaustion, And It's The Best Thing That Could Have Happened To Me* https://medium.com/thrive-global/10-years-ago-i-collapsed-from-burnout-and-exhaustion-and-its-the-best-thing-that-could-have-b1409f16585d

Part 3

Stephen R. Covey (2013) *The 7 Habits of Highly Effective People: Powerful Lessons in Personal Change* Covey, Stephen R.

Chapter 6

National Library of Medicine (2013) *Neuroanatomy, Reticular Activating System* https://www.ncbi.nlm.nih.gov/books/NBK549835/

NRP (2020) *Understanding Unconscious Bias* https://www.npr.org/2020/07/14/891140598/understanding-unconscious-bias

Forbes (2015) *Entrepreneurial Addiction Is A Real Problem: Here Are The 6 Warning Signs* https://www.forbes.com/sites/amymorin/2015/09/24/entrepreneurial-addiction-is-a-real-problem-here-are-the-6-warning-signs

Acknowledgements

Writing a book is not a solo (or duo) journey. There are so many people that helped bring this book to life! A very special thank you to the following people for helping us get this message and the work we do into a format that can now make a wider impact.

Every word matters when it comes to changing the current landscape of business to break the cycles of old-school hardcore hustle culture so that we can all live healthier, happier lives... while still having kick-ass businesses we love.

Thank you to the people who shared their stories of healthy (and unhealthy) hustle so openly in these pages. Because of your openness, others can now see stories of how business and life can be if they start to make the 1% changes laid out in this book.

Donna, who without our lunch by the water this book may still be an idea in the ether waiting to happen, and where the concept of Healthy Hustle was born. Thank you.

Janine, your generosity and dedication in making this book the best it can be is so appreciated and valued. We love having you in our corner.

Leah, your openness and care in sharing your knowledge, expertise and journalist eye has been everything.

Ali, you've been with us since the very beginning, we appreciate you! Thank you for being the very first to purchase this book.

Ellie, your brand magic continues to shine through.

Karen, your enthusiasm and support means the world to us.

ACKNOWLEDGEMENTS

A special thank you to our partners and family for supporting us throughout this journey (and beyond).

Nicky – Thank you Jules for always being my rock. Always believing in me and seeing what I can do, before I can even see and believe it myself. For always celebrating my quirkiness and for always laughing with me. For being my best friend and for all that you do. To my Mum Violet, Dad Dom, Sisters Haley and Monique – for being my cheerleaders throughout my whole life and always championing and believing in me. To the women in my family, Anyukám, Evi, Verus and Neni (Ica). Your strength, tenacity, determination runs through my veins in all that I do. My Hungarian Sisters (I'm looking at you Monika & Babette) and I are incredibly lucky to stand on shoulders of giants like you. To the outside world the Miklós women might come across as direct and head strong (some may say bossy), but we will never stop being aggressively helpful x

Ness – To my parents, Peter and Judy thank you for always supporting me. From a young girl with a bossy streak (I prefer 'leadership' to bossy) you encouraged me to follow my dreams in every stage of life. Even when the result of following my dreams didn't go to plan, you've always been there to pick up the pieces (as have you Wendy). To my kids Cam and Bec, you wore the brunt of my early days in business whilst I was deep in hustle trying to find the 'healthy' part. Your unconditional love and support means the world to me. My sister Janine, thanks for being my debriefing partner for everything. To my partner Wayne, you have been a huge supporter from day one, thank you for seeing me for who I am at my core. And finally, to Nicky – you are my business partner, best friend and greatest champion. I could not imagine doing business without you!